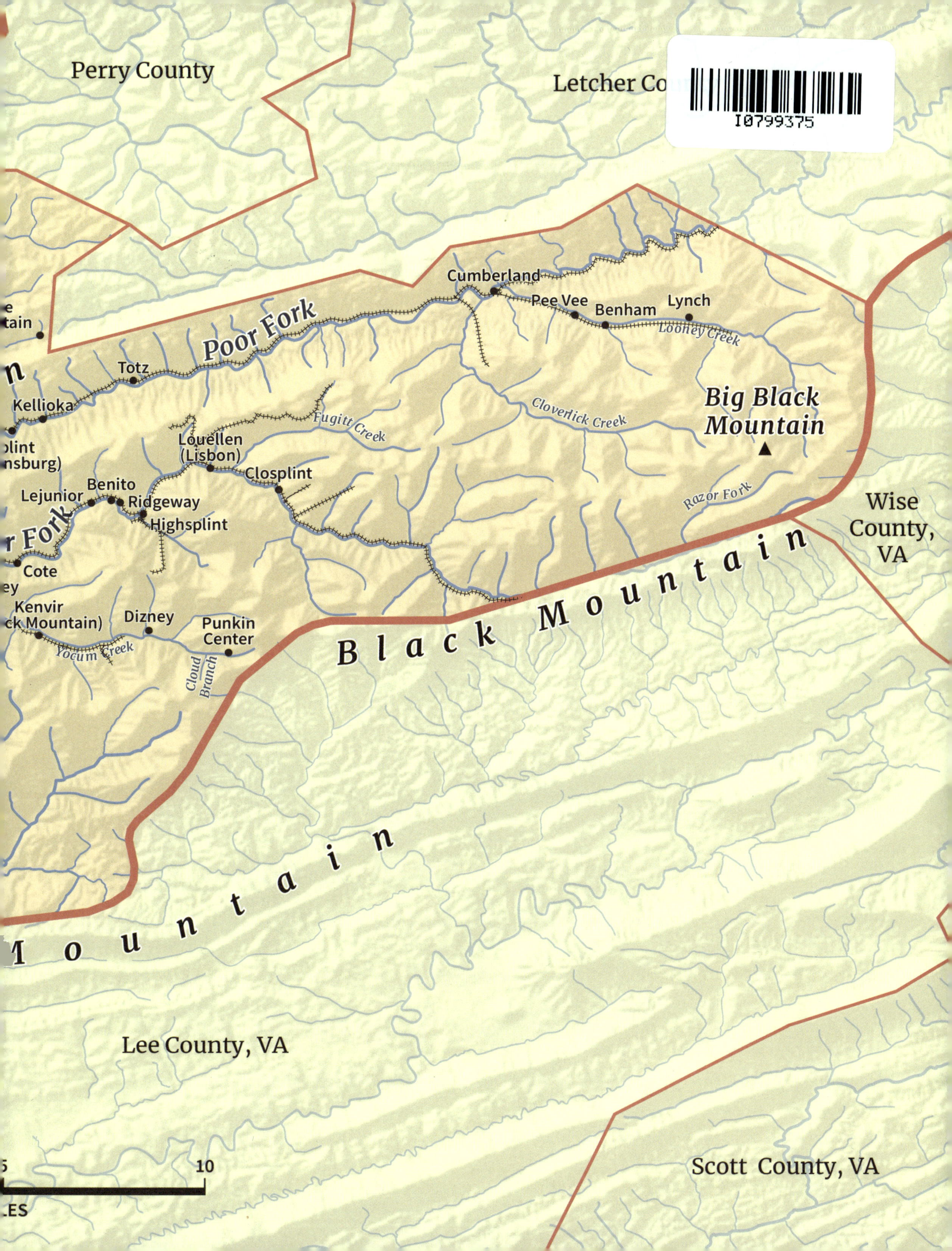

Perry County
Letcher Co
Cumberland
Pee Vee
Benham
Lynch
Looney Creek
Poor Fork
Totz
Kellioka
Big Black Mountain
Cloverlick Creek
Fugitt Creek
Louellen (Lisbon)
Closplint
Benito
Lejunior
Ridgeway
Highsplint
Razor Fork
Cote
Kenvir
Dizney
Punkin Center
Yocum Creek
Cloud Branch
Wise County, VA
Black Mountain
Lee County, VA
Scott County, VA
10

SCRIP

SCRIP

HOW THE COAL COMPANIES IMPOVERISHED HARLAN COUNTY

CHARLES EDWARD THOMAS

COUNTY LINE BOOKS

County Line Books
Asheville, North Carolina

First Edition

ISBN 979-8-9905448-0-2 (casebound)

ISBN 979-8-9905448-1-9 (ebook)

Edited by Peter Greggut
Maps by Olha Bosenko
Memorial photographs by Starr Sariego
Additional photographs by Ken Allen
Book design by Peggy Stockdale

Jacket images: (front) Ken Allen, (back) Lee Russell
Author photo: Claudia Piper

Printed in South Korea

www.harlanscrip.com

for Laura

Shady Grove, my little love,
Shady Grove, my darlin',
Shady Grove, my little love,
I'm going back to Harlan.

–Traditional

CONTENTS

INTRODUCTION

The word "scrip" comes to us directly from economics, where it means any document that says the bearer is entitled to receive something of value. It's an expansive term that applies to a variety of financial instruments, including IOUs. In this book, however, we will use the word in its narrower sense of the payment coal miners received in lieu of cash. Other low-wage industries, notably lumber and textiles, also used scrip, though not on the scale that was seen in the coal camps.

Many people think scrip was only rarely used. This book tests that theory by assembling photographs of all the known scrip from just a single sample area: Harlan County, Kentucky, where I was born and raised. My mother gave me a couple of pieces of scrip when I was young, and then many years later I started seeing it at flea markets and bought a few pieces. I remember stopping at a market near Pineville and picking up a Harlan County piece. An older man standing nearby gestured toward the scrip and said, "I must have spent that quarter a hundred times." I've always regretted not buying it and giving it to him.

A few years ago I started buying some of the more common (and cheaper) pieces and built up a collection of 100 or so tokens, all from Harlan County. I leave the rare ones to others; in support of this project, fellow collectors have generously shared photographs of their own holdings. All told, this book contains photographs of about 800 different pieces of scrip from 110 mining companies scattered across 58 Harlan County communities. And what I found is that almost all coal companies in the county used scrip. Only one large mine—International Harvester's operation at Benham—did not. But every member of the Harlan County Coal Operators Association used scrip.

In fact, the scrip system was used extensively in the U.S. coal industry between 1880 and 1950. This was true across large swaths of West Virginia and eastern Kentucky, but scrip could also be found in 34 other states. By the time the Harlan County coalfields were opened in 1910, the system had already been developed and was widely implemented.

Coal scrip typically consisted of brass, nickel or copper tokens with denominations matching U.S. coinage. The company name was stamped into the tokens, and they were usually also labeled "Good for Merchandise Only." In some cases, paper tokens were used, or even just notations in the company's books. But whatever its physical form, scrip could be spent only at the company store, or commissary, as these facilities were known in the coalfields.

In many coal camps, miners were forced to shop there, a policy that proved very profitable for the operators. Prices were higher in the company store, sometimes by as much as 15% or even 20%. The companies bought essentials such as flour, beans and cornmeal wholesale by the ton and resold them by the pound at greatly inflated markups. Getting paid a dollar that was actually worth 80 cents had the same effect on purchasing power as a 20% wage cut.

When laws were eventually passed outlawing direct payment in scrip, the coal companies came up with a workaround that accomplished the same thing: Scrip would be issued as an advance on wages. Paying miners not weekly but every two weeks, or even monthly, increased the likelihood that they would need to draw some scrip.

To provide for their loved ones, miners needed every cent they made. A single day off because of sickness—or, worse yet, a brief layoff—could mean no food on the table. It was a rare family indeed that didn't need to request scrip ahead of payday.

To further ensure that the company spent as little on wages as possible, coal companies extracted a wide range of deductions from the miners' theoretical earnings. Surviving pay stubs show that after docking workers for things like rent, lights, coal, insurance, bathhouse and smithing as well as scrip, there was little left. The remainder would have to serve for the entire pay period, and if it didn't, the miner would have to draw still more scrip—which would, of course, come out of the subsequent payday.

This was an essential aspect of the industry's strategy. It was one thing for a single family to go hungry for the last few days of the pay period, but if the entire workforce were left without food, it would risk triggering an outright rebellion. Thus, scrip was also a safety valve that enabled the work to continue with fewer disruptions.

When I see a $1 piece of scrip, I know that this "dollar" was paid to a miner who could buy perhaps 80 cents worth of food with it—and that dollar would go, not to some member of the local community, but directly back to the company that issued it. Instead of an honest dollar, what the miner got for his backbreaking labor was a trinket worth significantly less. The camp was a closed system, and this false currency cycled endlessly between the miners and the company store. If you have a piece of scrip from the mine where your grandfather worked, it's quite likely that he once held it in his hand.

In most of the mountain counties, the mines are closed now, and the entrances have been dynamited. Most of the shoddy camp houses have turned to dust, and in some places, even the railroad tracks have been removed. Even in some of the most productive areas, few traces of the coal industry remain. The scrip survives, though, preserved by a small group of patient collectors who have lovingly saved and cataloged these artifacts over many decades. It is their efforts that enable us to comprehend the full extent, and thus the consequences, of the scrip system.

Scrip is the physical evidence of subsistence wages.

If workers were paid a living wage, they could live on their earnings. Their paydays were too small to carry them over to the next one, so they had to draw scrip. Far from being rare, scrip was common. And the impact of subsistence wages spread far beyond the coal counties themselves, as the companies also drew workers from surrounding areas. Most of the men who spent their prime working years in the mines left with nothing. Only toward the end of the coal boom, when unionization, or the threat of it, resulted in higher wages and a livable income, did coal mining become sustainable for the workers.

Today, reports from the coal counties routinely identify the mine closures as the cause of the poverty that's so prevalent in West Virginia and eastern Kentucky. I contend, however, that the industry itself was a major cause of persistent mountain poverty. Using dubious strategies to acquire the mineral and land rights, gobbling up the available workforce, housing those workers in "towns" totally owned and controlled by the coal companies, and then compounding the problems by consistently paying subsistence wages effectively impoverished two or three generations of coal miners.

Lured by the promise of good jobs with housing provided, miners came by the thousands. Arriving by train, they were escorted to their homes in the coal camps and told that they could get supplies at the company store. But while the pay they were promised might have been barely adequate, what they actually received fell far short of that.

The housing was a trap. If a miner was laid off, he could be told to leave. If he was injured, the company would wait only so long before repossessing the property. If he was fired, he and his family became homeless. And since the company owned every house in town, it meant they were forced out of their community as well. This system did exactly what it was designed to do: Deter miners from forming a union. Conditions would have to be really bad for these workers to risk firing and eviction, but as we will see, that's exactly what happened.

To ensure their control of the county, the mine operators corrupted Harlan County's political system, buying votes and bribing the sheriff, the judge and the commonwealth attorney. They deputized the mine guards, many of whom had criminal records, and these hired thugs engaged in coercion, assault and even murder to keep the unions out. When all that did not suffice, these companies called on the state government which, over and over, sent in the National Guard to put down the inevitable strikes.

Harlan's labor history has been told time and again, and those accounts differ only in the details from what played out in the other coal mining counties. For the most part, this same book could have been written about any of those areas in eastern Kentucky or West Virginia. The pattern of hunger, strikes and repression repeated itself all across the mountain counties. The following pages sketch some of that shared story.

CHAPTER 1

THE MOST BEAUTIFUL COUNTRY WE HAVE SEEN YET

On a trip in June 1908, Franklin Delano Roosevelt wrote to his wife, Eleanor.

> *If you can imagine a succession of ridges, each fifteen hundred or so feet above the valleys, running up at a very precipitous angle and covered with marvelous trees and an undergrowth of rhododendrons and holly you can get a general idea of the country–the path was just about the steepest kind that I would care to take a horse up, following generally a water course filled with boulders and ledges of rock.*
>
> *We got to the top of the Cumberland Mountain about 10 o'clock and had one of the most magnificent views I have ever seen, looking to the south over the angle of Virginia almost to the mountains of North Carolina and Tennessee, and to the Northward over the Harlan County, Kentucky, section that Uncle Warren and Davis are interested in...*
>
> *We rode into Harlan again in time for lunch and are now ensconced here, saddle bags and all, at Judge Lewis' Hotel. This afternoon we are just back from a ride of five or six miles up Martin Fork, the most beautiful country we have seen yet. The sides of the valley going up 2,000 feet, heavily wooded with great poplars, chestnuts and a dozen or two other deciduous trees and every mile or so a fertile bottom with fine crops and a stream of splendid water.*[1]

The Roosevelts had been married only three years at the time of this trip and they wrote each other often, sometimes several times a day. Then an attorney, FDR had come to Harlan to help his uncle, Warren Delano Jr., with the legal work of clearing titles. Even a simple property transfer requires time, money and legal expertise, and the work they'd undertaken was far more involved. Multiple heirs and errors in the records of deeds made it difficult and time-consuming.

In 1870, Philadelphia businessman Edward M. Davis bought 86,000 acres in and near Harlan County, all of it steep and forested. Forty years later, his son Charles Davis and Delano Jr. were back on one of several trips they took to the area. Through dozens of lawsuits, they cleared title to 75,000 acres, mostly in Harlan County. The trip these lawyers made was one of hundreds to the region by similar legal teams to prepare for the coming coal boom.[2]

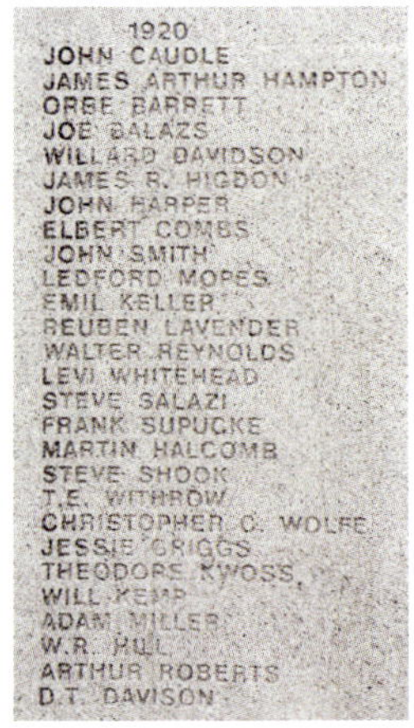

By the late 19th century, it was widely known that eastern Kentucky contained an estimated 35 billion tons of coal. The counties of Johnson, Floyd, Pike, Letcher, Harlan, Bell, Knox, Perry, Knott, Leslie, Clay, Martin and Breathitt were particularly rich. All told, about 13,000 square miles (8.3 million acres) of Kentucky land had coal deposits. West Virginia held even more, also concentrated in a dozen or so counties.

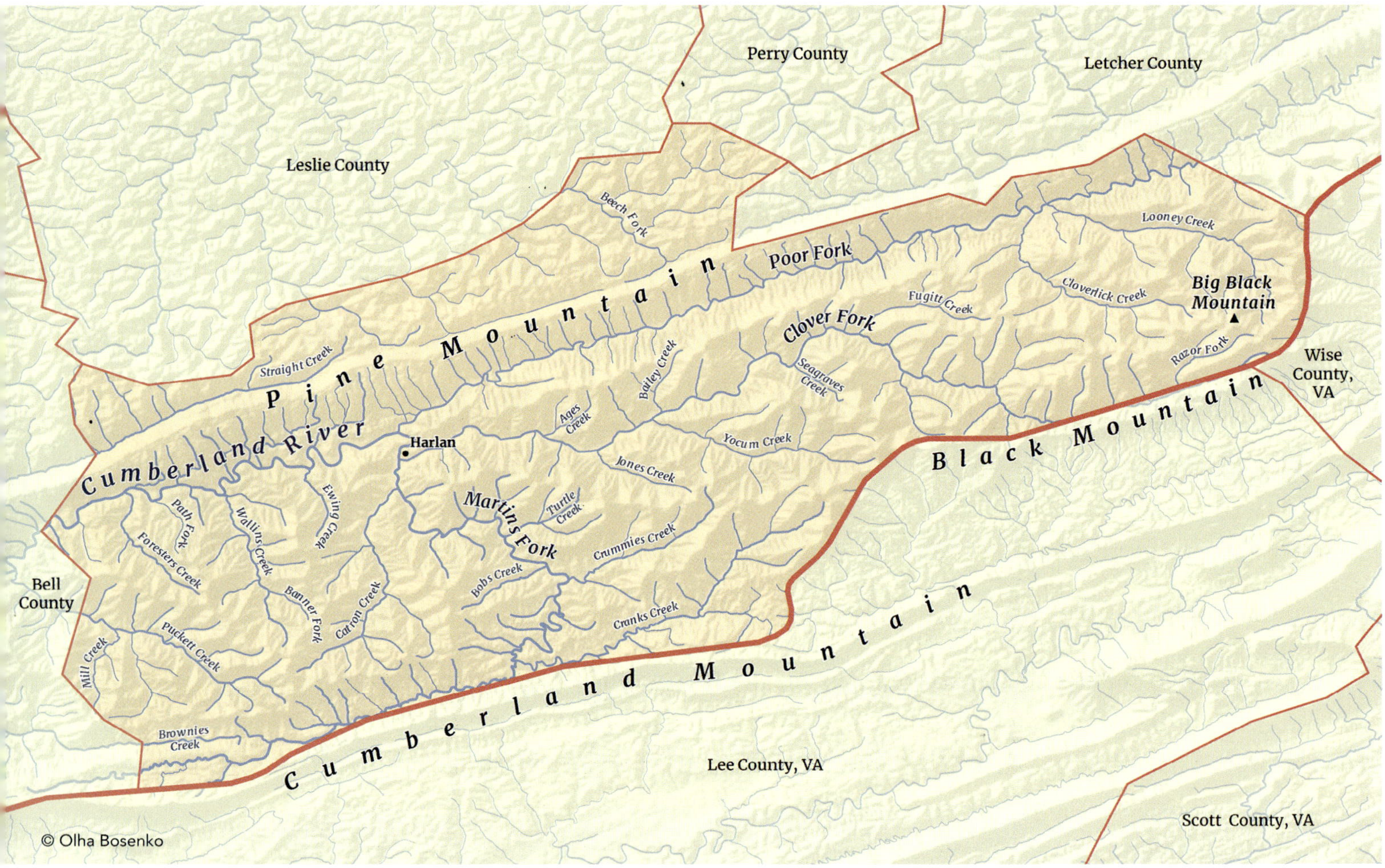

The headwaters of the Cumberland River are in Harlan County where Clover Fork, Martins Fork and Poor Fork converge to form the river.

Between 1880 and 1910, individuals and corporations formed companies to buy up the coal lands in both states, either purchasing acreage outright or securing the mineral rights. For these businesses, the coal itself came cheap, the rights to it having been obtained by a range of questionable legal tactics including the broad form deed, the Mayo form, the use of quitclaim deeds, and forced partition sales.

Davis and Delano Jr. were shareholders in the Kentenia Corp., having put up the $10 million that funded the company's property acquisitions. Although Kentenia (derived from the state names Kentucky, Tennessee and Virginia) did operate mines of its own, its primary function was to lease the mineral rights it had acquired to other companies that would actually extract the coal, in exchange for a fee for each ton that was mined.

Delano Jr. served on the board of the Louisville & Nashville Railroad, and he actively pushed a plan to build a line into Harlan County, understanding that as soon as it was finished, the value of the coal leasees would skyrocket. In 1910, just two years after FDR's trip, the L&N tracks reached the town of Harlan, and soon made their way up Clover Fork, Poor Fork and Martins Fork.[3]

Drilling and blasting into the mountains began immediately. Within a few years more than 100 firms—coal companies, steel mills, utilities, coke makers and coal gasification plants—had begun operations, pockmarking the county with mines. Ford Motor Co., U.S. Steel, Peabody Energy, Wisconsin Steel, Koppers Co., International Harvester and Chicago Edison all owned coal mines in Harlan County. These companies eagerly took advantage of the coming of the railroad to establish or buy mines in this newly opened coal-rich area, eventually extracting hundreds of millions of tons of coal from Harlan County alone—all of it dug by workers who were paid the absolute minimum required to sustain life.

In 1910 Harlan County's population was 10,000. To meet the growing need for workers, coal company agents first recruited men from neighboring states, notably Alabama, and then broadened their search to the nation's ports. There, they would meet ships arriving from Europe, promising good jobs with housing provided. U.S. Steel's mine at Lynch once noted that over 25 languages were spoken in its coal camp, and materials

(continued on p.11)

The Lords and Ladies of the Coalfields

In 1911 the Louisville and Nashville Railroad (L&N) reached Coxton, and the corporations developing the Harlan coalfield dispatched an excursion train to celebrate. Coxton was the site of two mines. One was Melcroft Coal Company, owned by the Mellon family of Pittsburg. The Melcroft company store was called Chestnut Ridge Supply Co. The Mellons owned or financed dozens of major companies including Alcoa, Gulf Oil, Westinghouse, and the giant coal producer, Koppers, which owned the second mine. Koppers owned over 200 coal mines, most in West Virginia, and now one in Coxton.

The identity of those on the train has been lost to history, but it is safe to say that officials of the L&N, the Kentenia Corporation, and Koppers were on board. Members of the Continental Miners Band from Arjay, Kentucky in Bell County are at the left, and on the end at the right are the train's engineer and brakeman. Eleanor Roosevelt can be seen under the word "First". She's in the second row in a white hat, standing alone in the crowd.

Chestnut Ridge was the company store for Mellon's mine, Melcroft

Courtesy of Steve Cawood

(continued from p.7)

for workers were published in six of those languages. By 1930, eastern Kentucky and West Virginia had seen massive population growth; Harlan County alone was home to some 64,000 people—a more than fivefold increase in 20 years.

The mines' output helped fuel the Industrial Revolution, producing a legion of new millionaires. Large companies grew larger, some—such as Koppers and Peabody—becoming true energy goliaths. Companies including Ford and U.S. Steel operated what were called "captive mines," meaning that they used the coal in their own factories, rather than selling it.

The product was good quality—low ash, high energy content—and the mining methods of the time were well suited to steep mountainsides. Miners drilled into seemingly endless coal seams, inserted an explosive, lit the fuse and subsequently shoveled the broken coal into cars. Mules or electric winches pulled the cars out of the mouth of the mine and dumped the coal into chutes that fed the tipple.

Tipples dumped the cleaned and sorted coal into gondolas that could hold up to 100 tons each; the long trains then hauled them away, mostly north. Coal-powered engines pulled the coal to Chicago Edison, to Ford's River Rouge plant at Dearborn, Michigan, and to factories across the country.

Coal was king back then. Most homes and businesses were heated with it and coal gas was the most common fuel for lighting. Rail transportation had long depended on coal. Oceangoing steamships ran on coal until they converted to oil during World War I. Factories powered by electricity used their own coal-fed generators to produce it, as did streetcar companies and electric railways. Chicago Edison and other utilities were rapidly moving toward more centralized power generation and the creation of a nationwide electrical grid.

The Harlan deposits were vast and the coal, being low in ash and sulfur, was ideal for making coke, a key resource for steel production. The steel industry was growing fast and thus needed ever larger amounts of coal.

"We came from Walker County, Alabama, where my father was in the coal business," coal operator Bryan Whitfield told an interviewer. "He did prospecting here in the county in 1903. In 1907, he went to Straight Creek

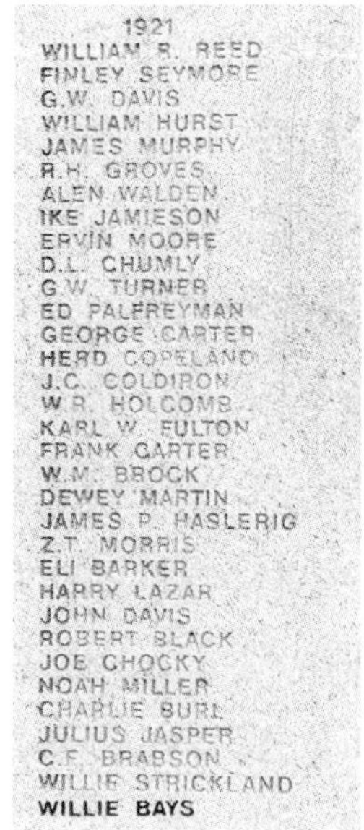

[in Bell County] and developed the Left Fork Coal Co., two mines there, ArJay and Glendon. He sold out to Continental Coal Co. in 1911 and came to Harlan and developed the Clover Fork Coal Co. at Kitts, above Harlan. We bought this property from T.J. [Asher].[4]

"Mr. Bob Creech ... developed the first big mine on Wallins Creek in 1911. And the second mine was White Star near Wilhoit. The third mine was Wisconsin Steel, Benham, International Harvester. The fourth mine was Clover Fork Coal Co., which was my father and uncle's operation, and they were ready to load coal when the railroad got there."[5]

In 1920 Bryan Whitfield opened his own mine, Harlan Collieries Company, at Brookside. He became a leader in the Harlan County Coal Operators Association.

Mine after mine opened in Harlan. Seeing a chance to further expand their fortunes, the financial titans of the day invested heavily.

J.P. Morgan's U.S. Steel spent more than $5 million (equivalent to over $110 million today) to create Lynch, Harlan County's largest coal town. Named after the company's president, its facilities included the tipple, commissary, a bathhouse, worker housing, and even a hotel.[6]

Henry Ford, recognizing that there was more profit to be made by eliminating the middleman, sought independence from supply chains. Accordingly, he started his own steel mills, which needed coal by the trainload. To provide it, Ford bought 16 coal mines, including one at Banner Fork in Harlan County. He had given the name Fordson to his line of trucks and tractors and he called the mine Fordson as well.

Heinrich Koppers had developed a new way to manufacture coke, and his 38-acre site in St. Paul, Minnesota, needed ever more coal to meet increasing demand.

In the 1840s, Cyrus McCormick began manufacturing the horse-drawn reaper that he, his father, and an enslaved man named Jo Anderson had invented. In 1902, with financing from J.P. Morgan, McCormick's son oversaw a merger with several other companies to form International Harvester. The massive new firm produced farm equipment, trucks and automobiles. Harvester opened a mine at Benham to power its subsidiary, Wisconsin Steel.

Samuel Insull, a former assistant to Thomas Edison, ran Chicago Edison beginning in 1892, and by 1894 it was the largest power company in the city. His strategy for growth involved buying up as much of the competition as he could and relentlessly reducing customers' costs—temporarily, at least—to further ensure that the company achieved dominance in the industry.

Some owners named the mines and the camps for their wives and daughters—Mary Helen, Mary Alice, Louellen, Alva, Lena Rue, Twila. Samuel Insull named his coal camp after himself. In one case the coal operator named the camp Lejunior after his infant son, Lee Bowling Jr.[7]

By 1920, there were more than 30 Harlan County mines employing 4,000 men. Over the next decade, another 50 mines were added, employing an additional 11,000 miners. Coal was so profitable that even during the Great Depression a dozen new mines came on line, employing 3,000 more men.

Coal was a mature industry, and these companies sent experienced managers to develop and run the mines. Their top priority, after the mine itself, was the coal camp. It was a low-wage industry and safety precautions were rare. As a result, strikes were common even when union organizers were not involved. As we will see, the camps were designed from the start to discourage and defeat attempts to organize.

1926

1929

1934

Samuel Insull

Chicago-based industrialist Samuel Insull consolidated the Midwest power grid. He partnered with J.P. Morgan and the Vanderbilts to buy up companies that generated electricity and run them with coal from eight mines he owned outright. Insull bought so much coal from Peabody Coal Co. that some people referred to the Kenvir mining operation as Peabody-Insull.

Insull appeared on the cover of *Time* magazine three times. In 1926 he was featured because of the electrical empire he had built that was fueled by Kentucky coal. He made the cover again in 1929 when he built Chicago's Civic Opera House, an opulent venue housed in a brand-new 42-story building.

Trading on his name recognition and reputation, Insull made tens of millions of dollars selling worthless stock to investors. Hundreds of thousands of people lost their life savings. He fled the country, going first to Paris. But when France agreed to extradite him, Insull moved on and was eventually extradited from Turkey, prompting the 1934 *Time* cover that showed him hiding his face.

Floyd Thompson, the most famous attorney of his day, represented Insull, using a "They all do it" defense. Thompson maintained that although Insull had repeatedly violated the law, he had behaved the same as other major corporations—and the jury acquitted him of all charges.[8]

(AP photo)

Henry Ford, the owner of the Fordson mine at Banner Fork, was a long-time fascist. He idolized Adolph Hitler and published an anti-Semitic weekly newspaper, *The Dearborn Independent*. Ford distributed the paper through his car dealerships and to his employees, and its circulation was second only to the *New York Daily News*. In this photograph from 1938, two Nazi officials presented him with the Grand Cross of the German Eagle.

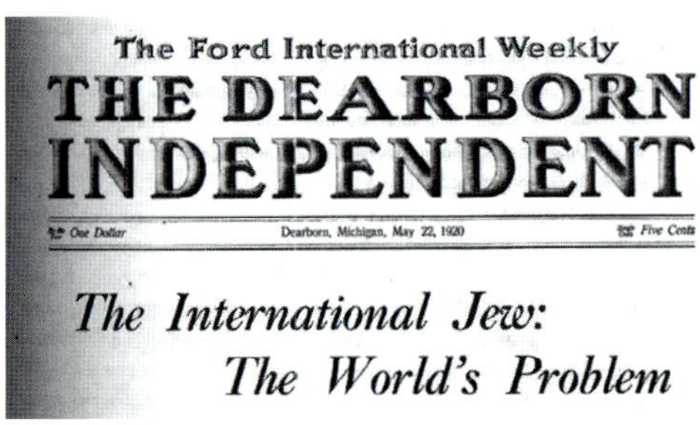

The Ford International Weekly

THE DEARBORN INDEPENDENT

One Dollar — Dearborn, Michigan, May 22, 1920 — Five Cents

The International Jew: The World's Problem

Library of Congress

CHAPTER 2

THE COAL CAMPS

> In 1913 the coal fields of southern Colorado were only nominally in the United States. In every practical sense they were controlled by the operators. Houses, stores, churches, streets, towns, land, were company-owned. Company guards policed the streets and enforced the law of the operators. Guards were stationed on the outskirts of some towns to investigate the credentials of strangers wishing to enter. Miners leased only the right of entry to their houses, so that the company could prohibit anyone it pleased from visiting the occupants. Miners were paid not in United States currency, but in company scrip, in defiance of the law.
>
> – *John Greenway*[9]

As it was in Colorado, so it was in Harlan. The operators had engineered a system to mine coal as cheaply as possible and they employed it everywhere.

In 1918, Chicago's Peabody Coal Co. opened its Black Mountain Corp. mine on the upper stretch of Yocum Creek, armed with a contract from Chicago Edison to buy all the coal the company could produce. As Hal King has written,[10] Peabody had bought Jesse Farley's farm in 1916 to be used as the site of the coal camp the company would name Kenvir, combining the first letters of Kentucky and Virginia. Over the next two years, Peabody built more than 500 frame houses, office buildings, a coal processing tipple, a bathhouse, repair shops, a scale and a company store. Men poured into the camp with their families, ready to start new jobs to improve their lives.

Everything in the town belonged to the company, and the mine superintendent was its undisputed ruler. There were no elections for mayor because there was no mayor. The super's word was law, and if you didn't like it you could leave. The county sheriff was cooperative, deputizing the company's guards. As we will see, Black Mountain guards would be involved in many of the armed conflicts that made national news.

To supplement the armed guards, it wasn't unusual for the camps to be surrounded by fencing. Some had guard shacks or towers at the entrance. Kenvir, however, had no need of fences. The only way in or out was down the road through Evarts. Going the other way, up the mountain, the road ended at Punkin Center, two miles short of the Virginia line. This geography played a key role in the Battle of Evarts, which turned out to be the turning point in the county's coal war.

In the 1930s, steel cables were used to lock the entrance gate at the Louellen coal camp, on Clover Fork, owned by the Cornett-Lewis Coal Co.:

> They had a big post on each side, [where] you pulled off the highway and went over into the camp; they put a big crosstie on each side of the road, and they had a steel rope stretched across there, and they kept a lock on it. And if you see any people come, you had to alert the watchmen, and they'd let you in and he'd lock it back.
>
> –*Lloyd Lefevre*

> They had guards to let you in and guards to let you out. Like a concentration camp or something. And we grew up under those conditions. You didn't get *in* that camp without permission and you didn't get *out* of that camp without permission.
>
> –*Julia Cowans*[11]

The company town of Verda featured a guardhouse perched in a large tree beside the road. Residents recall seeing machine guns displayed there and on the butcher block in the commissary.[12] Over at Lynch, the fences were used to keep out union organizers. Several people have reported that as soon as they entered the camp, they were challenged by company guards and had to justify their presence.

The Company Store

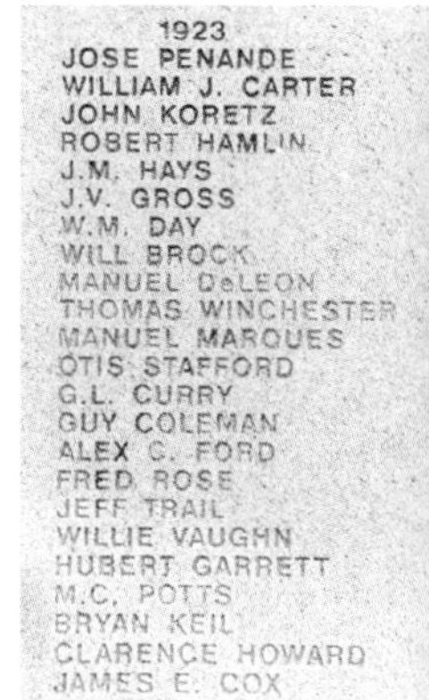

In 1930, an appeals court judge described Kenvir, a typical company town:

> The appellant Black Mountain Corporation owns extensive coal lands in Harlan County, and in 1918 it constructed a mining camp on Yocum Creek. This mining camp is now known as Kenvir and has a population of approximately 2,500. It is unincorporated, and the Black Mountain Corporation owns substantially all the real property in and around the town. When the camp was established, streets and roads were laid out; but these are the private property of the Black Mountain Corporation and are used by the public only with its permission.[13]

The judge did not elaborate, but the referenced "real property" included a company store—the only store in town and the only one that would accept the scrip that the workers there received.

Miners and their families at the PV&K Coal Company store, Lejunior, Kentucky, September, 1946

Department of the Interior

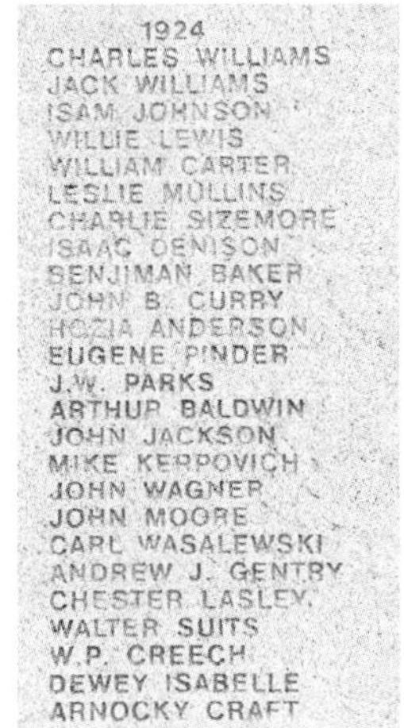

Camps were isolated, laws varied from state to state, and companies varied in the extent to which they chose to follow whatever laws there were. Over time, those laws changed. But even when workers weren't paid directly in scrip, most still needed it in order to buy food and other essential items. And that meant surrendering a portion of their theoretical cash wages in exchange for scrip.

In places where other shopping options were available, coal operators used various strategies to pressure workers to buy their groceries at the company store, thereby ensuring that a chunk of the miners' wages would revert to the employer even before payday came. In a 1932 essay, Melvin P. Levy quoted a letter from the Black Mountain Corp. to John Burton, a miner in the company's employ:

> Dear Sir:
>
> On checking our pay rolls and books in the store we find that you are not drawing very much scrip. This is evidence to us that you are trading with the independent stores... We're furnishing your employment and pay you twice a month for your earned wages.
>
> I am sure that things can be adjusted and you will give us one-hundred per cent of your trade.[14]

In another instance, the superintendent of the Clover Fork mine at Kitts told an employee, "If you trade at Piggly Wiggly you can get your job at Piggly Wiggly."[15]

Most Harlan County mines used the "room and pillar method," in which large pillars of coal are left in place to support the roof. Eventually the pillars are removed to gain access to that coal. Called "retreat mining," or "robbing," this was dangerous work: At some point, the roof would collapse. Not surprisingly, robbing was nobody's favorite.

The miners understood full well all of the ways that they were being taken advantage of. Consider this story from Black Mountain:

> These two men approached the mine superintendent, J.J. Asbury, looking for a job. He told 'em, "We don't have nothing right now but robbin' work." They knew what he was talking about, but one of them said, "Well, we never did no work in a company store before, but we're willing to give it a try."[16]

Deductions

The low pay—miners called it "starvation wages"—kept them from ever owning much of value. No house, no car, no savings, just living from payday to payday and never getting ahead. Paying on a home is typically the main way workers of any kind build what's called "generational wealth": Assets that can be passed down to their children, helping to ensure that they'll be better off than their parents were.

Although the main deduction from the miners' pay was for scrip, there were also many others, ensuring that little actual cash found its way into the pay envelope. And while drawing scrip was theoretically voluntary, the cumulative effect of all these charges was to make sure the workers received so little money that they had to ask for advances, which were payable only in scrip.

Management consultant Peter Drucker coined the phrase "profit center" in 1945, and the concept has since been widely embraced. Airlines, for example, used to provide luggage check-in as a service; now it's a profit center. The coal companies, though, were using this strategy long before that.

Car checks. Miners who were paid by the ton attached brass tags with their number on them to the coal cars to get credit for the coal they mined. From the author's collection

If there was a doctor on call in the coal camps there'd be a deduction, regardless of whether a particular worker needed treatment. Deducting 88 cents per miner per month might not seem like much, but multiply that by hundreds of employees over a number of years and it adds up. The doctor was paid a set salary and the rest fed the company's bottom line.

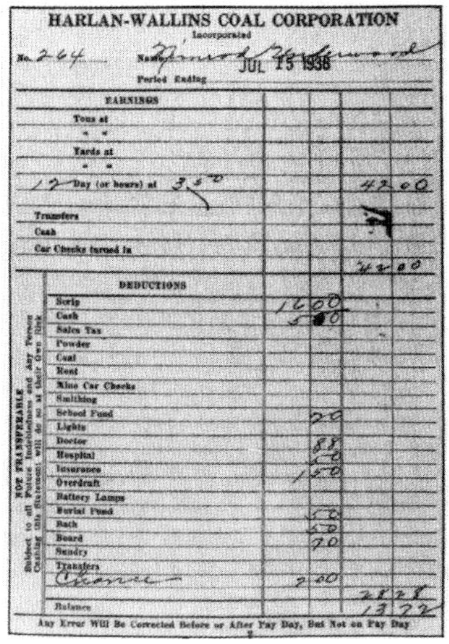

Note the deduction of $2 for "Chance" at the bottom

In addition, companies erected rows of identical tar paper-sided houses for the workers and deducted the rent—usually $2 per room per month—from their pay. Cheap to build, these flimsy structures helped ensure that construction costs were recouped in a very few years, after which housing the workers became another profit center.

If the company built a church in the camp, there would be a deduction to pay for it. Companies often paid all or part of the minister's salary as well, and management attended these churches alongside the miners. Under the circumstances, it would be a brave preacher indeed who voiced any criticism of his and his congregation's employer.

Special circumstances sometimes called for additional measures. U.S. Steel's mine at Lynch had so many Black workers that the camp featured three different Black churches. Because all of the foremen and company officials were white, they did not attend, and so couldn't monitor, what went on in those sanctuaries. Accordingly, the company found it necessary to remind the ministers not to allow union meetings on the premises.

A handwritten note inscribed on a 1934 letter from the treasurer of U.S. Coal & Coke Co. (owned by U.S. Steel) to Lynch mine Superintendent W.V. Whiteman spells out the policy in no uncertain terms. The letter concerns the leases for the churches in question and, in the note, the company instructs Whiteman to tell the ministers to use those facilities "for church purposes only and no other," with the principal words underlined for added emphasis.[17]

Sometimes, miners had to provide their own tools, chiefly picks and shovels. These were available at the commissary, along with the carbide that helped fuel the open-flame headlamps. There was even a deduction for "smithing"—sharpening the miner's pick.

Pearl Bassham owned the Harlan-Wallins Coal Corp. at Verda, as well as a used car lot in Harlan. Bassham would sometimes park a worn-out old car in front of the commissary, deduct $2 from each miner's pay, and draw a name to choose the winner of the car. He did not think it necessary to ask the men if they wanted to take part in the raffle.[18]

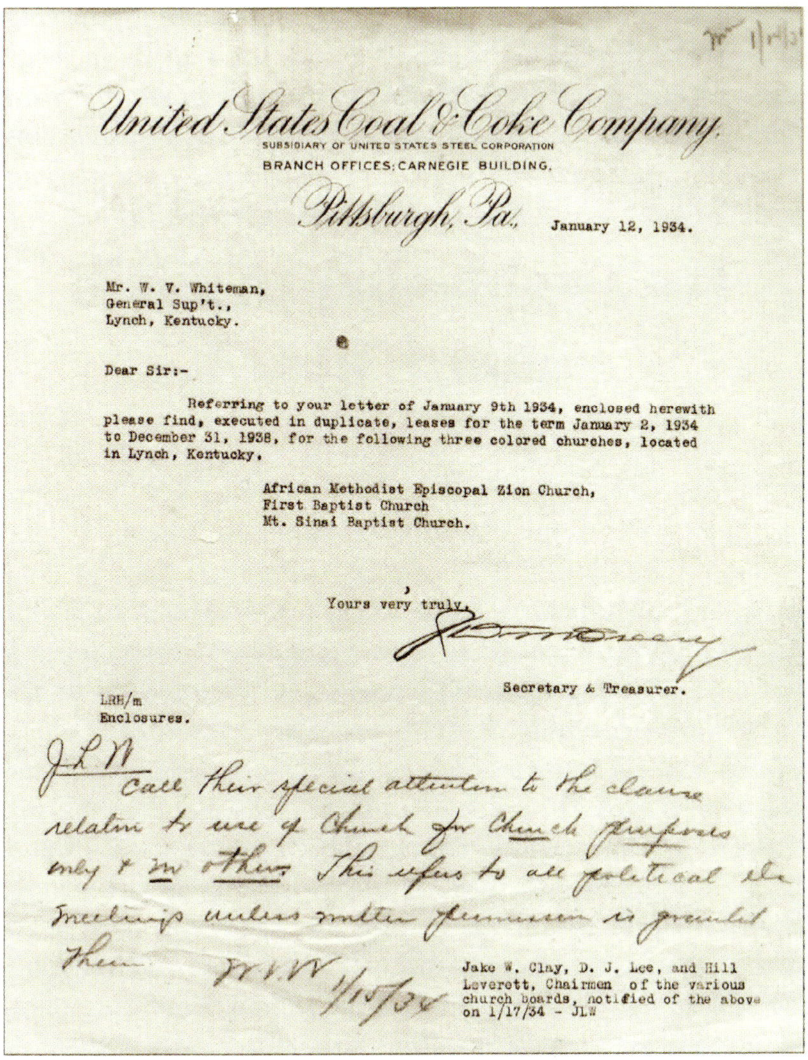

United States Coal & Coke Company
SUBSIDIARY OF UNITED STATES STEEL CORPORATION
BRANCH OFFICES: CARNEGIE BUILDING,
Pittsburgh, Pa., January 12, 1934.

Mr. W. V. Whiteman,
General Sup't.,
Lynch, Kentucky.

Dear Sir:-

Referring to your letter of January 9th 1934, enclosed herewith please find, executed in duplicate, leases for the term January 2, 1934 to December 31, 1938, for the following three colored churches, located in Lynch, Kentucky.

African Methodist Episcopal Zion Church,
First Baptist Church
Mt. Sinai Baptist Church.

Yours very truly,

Secretary & Treasurer.

LRH/m
Enclosures.

J.L.W.
Call their special attention to the clause relative to use of Church for Church purposes only & no other. This refers to all political etc. meetings unless written permission is granted them. W.V.W. 1/15/34

Jake W. Clay, D. J. Lee, and Hill Leverett, Chairmen of the various church boards, notified of the above on 1/17/34 - JLW

The handwritten note at the bottom reads, "J.L.W. Call their special attention to the clause relative to use of Church for Church purposes only & no other. This refers to all political, etc. meetings unless written permission is granted them. W.V.W, 1/15/34."

From *The Harlan Renaissance* by William H. Turner. Used with permission

Yellow Dog Contract

One of the ways the operators kept unions out was to require employees to sign a pledge not to join a labor union. Although they were coerced into signing, many miners felt bound by them. Others understood that signing under threat of job loss was not valid because it was not a contract that was entered into willingly. That's not just common sense, but a legal concept too.

This contract was required of employees as a condition of employment. When you were hired, you had to sign it. If you were already employed and refused to sign it, you were fired. It required that employees conform not just their actions, but their thoughts, to the company's will. "The employees will not join or belong... and will not aid, encourage or approve..." It's not enough to refrain from joining the union. You also have to disapprove of it!

In 1935 President Roosevelt signed the Wagner Act, which guaranteed the right to organize, and also outlawed blacklisting, yellow-dog contracts, and discrimination on the basis of union activity.

Expecting that the Supreme Court would overturn the act, some Harlan coal companies violated it. In 1937, when the Supreme Court upheld it instead, a Senate subcommittee on Civil Liberties, headed by Wisconsin Senator Robert M. La Follette, Jr., began hearings into labor practices in various industries.

Contract

In order to preserve to each man the right to do such work as he pleases and for whom he pleases and the right to payment in proportion to services rendered, to preserve the natural and constitutional right of individual contract, to preserve to each individual the fruits of his own labor and to promote the interest of both parties hereto

HARLAN-WALLINS COAL CORP., INCORPORATED

employer and .... employee, agree as follows:

That so long as the relation of employer and employee exists, between them, the employer will not knowingly employ, or keep in its employment, any member of the United Mine Workers of America, the I. W. W., or any other mine labor organization, and the employee will not join or belong to any such union or organization, and will not aid, encourage or approve the organization thereof, it being understood that the policy of said Company is to operate a non-union mine, and that it would not enter into any contract of employment under any other conditions; and if and when said relation of employer and employee, at any time and under any circumstances terminates, the employee agrees that he will not then or thereafter, in any manner, molest, annoy or interfere with the business, customers or employees of the employer, and will not aid or encourage anyone else in so doing.

Witness the following signatures, this the ...... day of ...., 193...

HARLAN-WALLINS COAL CORPORATION, INCORPORATED

By officer or agent ....
Employee ....
Witness ....

JOB REQUIREMENTS:

The yellow-dog contract that the Harlan-Wallins Coal Corp. required employees to sign. Such agreements, now illegal, barred employees from joining or supporting a union. Pearl Bassham, owned Harlan-Wallins, and Morris Saylor ran the company store in Molus. Saylor, who was also the county judge, had to sign off on deputy sheriff appointments. Among the 169 deputies he confirmed, 64 were indicted for felonies and 37 were felons. Sheriff Theodore Middleton was also in business with Bassham and Morris.

A swinging bridge on the Cumberland River at Wilhoit, 1929

CHAPTER 3

KEEP YOUR EYE UPON THE SCALE

In 1890, a hymn called "Life is Like a Mountain Railway" was written by M.E. Abbey and set to music by Charles Davis Tillman.

It began:

Life is like a mountain railway,
With an engineer that's brave.
You must make the run successful,
From the cradle to the grave.
Watch the curves, the fills, the tunnels;
Never falter, never quail;
Keep your hand upon the throttle,
And your eye upon the rail.

Appearing soon after recording had been invented, the song was an astounding success. Recorded dozens of times, it was sung in churches and concert halls alike. Everybody knew it, and it's still sung today in old-time music circles.

Nobody knows who changed the words, but the miners' version soon became as widely known as the original:

Miner's life is like a sailor's
'Board a ship to cross the waves.
Every day his life's in danger,
Still he ventures, being brave.

Watch the rocks, they're falling daily,
Careless miners often fail.
Keep your hand upon the dollar,
And your eye upon the scale.

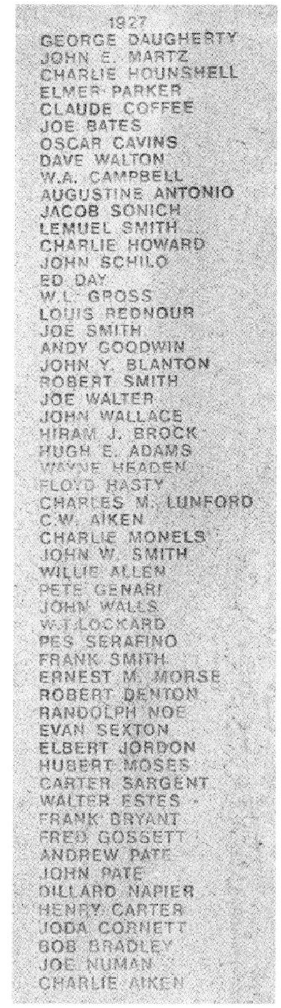

You've been docked and docked again boys,
You've been loading two to one;
Worn-out boots and worn-out miners,
Blackened lungs and children pale,
Keep your hand upon the dollar,
And your eye upon the scale.

Union miners, stand together,
Heed no operator's tale.
Keep your hand upon the dollar,
And your eye upon the scale.

These plain words reflected fundamental tensions in the employer/employee relationship. Owners used any means conceivable to reduce payroll in order to boost profits. Any reason might become an excuse to dock miners' pay: Too much slate in the coal, timbers not properly set. At the Brookside mine, Bryan Whitfield established a policy of paying less to miners who were under 25 years of age or over 50. The former were deemed inexperienced, and the latter were said to be worn out.[19]

As for "Keep your hand upon the dollar," paying miners in cash instead of scrip was one of the earliest union demands. And "Keep your eye upon the scale" was a further heads-up to workers, since cheating at the scales was common. An impartial "checkweighman" was another frequent union demand. In union mines, if they succeeded in getting it into the contract, workers had the right to elect, by secret ballot at the union meeting, their own checkweighman to oversee the company's man. Perhaps not surprisingly, when the company's man weighed the coal, the result always seemed to favor the owner.

The biggest offender in Harlan County was Pearl Bassham's Harlan-Wallins mine at Verda, where an inspector found that the scales had been doctored by the company to give short weight to the miners. The inspector calculated that the maneuver shorted the miners' pay by some 3,000 to 4,000 tons per month.

The operators required miners to perform some work with no pay at all. A single set of rails ran up to the face of the coal, where two empty cars would be delivered. The loaders filled the car nearest the coal face. They then had to transfer that coal to the other car and fill the near car again before both cars were hauled out. Since the miners were paid by the ton, they weren't paid for this "double bunking." Miners referred to the practice as "loading two for one," and they objected to it all across the coalfields.

Essential tasks such as shoring up the roof, laying track and cleaning up non-coal debris were also unpaid. The miners called this "dead work," and when they were able to organize, receiving payment for those jobs was high on the list of demands.

Another thing miners weren't paid for was the time it took to travel from the mine entrance to the coal face and back. This could be considerable, and the result was that miners wound up working longer hours than what they were theoretically putting in. "Portal to portal pay" was a frequent demand of striking workers.

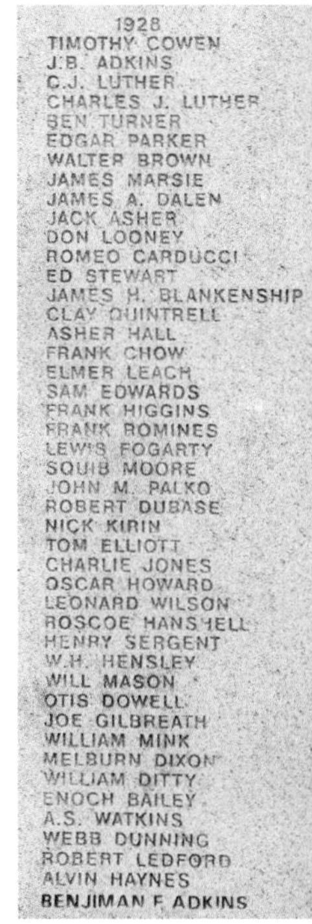

Fighting Back

The daily indignities of being blatantly cheated and of living in a "town" where they were almost totally devoid of rights took a heavy toll on the miners and their families. Mine superintendents, backed up by armed guards, wielded power that extended into every aspect of life. Self-respect required the miners to fight back at any opportunity, and from the very opening of the coalfields, strikes were frequent.

Operators quickly gained control over Harlan County government, and that gave them control of the local schools. I attended county schools from first grade through high school, and in all those years I remember unions being discussed exactly once. There was a strike going on, I think at Brookside, that was much in the news, and in my freshman history class one girl said something about the strikers being too lazy to work. I disputed her contention, and we all looked to the teacher to referee the dispute. Instead, he said: "We're not here to talk about that. Let's get back to history."

Even the post office was controlled by the operators. In most mining camps, the superintendent or commissary clerk was also the postmaster. Thus, "It was easy for the postmaster to serve the company by scanning incoming mail for radical literature or correspondence from labor leaders."[20]

The Harlan Daily Enterprise

Founded in 1903 as a booster paper, *The Harlan Daily Enterprise* was the coal operators' mouthpiece. When mine accidents were reported, employee error was the cause. The miners called the *Enterprise* a "scab paper," since it published the operators' opinions as fact, blamed work stoppages on outside agitators, and declined to report at all on things like unsafe conditions and low pay. And when mine operators tried to explain the frequent strikes, they tended to look everywhere except at their own pay scale and working conditions.

At the same time, the *Enterprise* leased the full wire of The Associated Press, so the paper's coverage of national and international events was often more balanced and quite thorough. The AP connection cut both ways, however. When the wire service picked up a Harlan County story, the coal company's version of the events was usually the one that would circulate nationwide. In times of great turmoil, however, the northern papers sometimes sent in their own reporters, so there was some independent national coverage.

According to the *Enterprise,* union organizing was the work of outsiders, often depicted as communists or socialists, who stirred up the miners. Alternately, it was sometimes presented as a conspiracy of Northern coal operators aiming to destroy the Southern coal industry. The dubious claim was that if unionization raised wages, Southern mines would no longer be able to compete with the Northern mines.[21] In fact, however, many Northern mines were unionized. Meanwhile, the other nearby paper, Bell County's *Pineville Sun*, urged officials to crush the union—without "too many scruples as to the methods."

Operators at seven Harlan County mines went further still, prohibiting miners outright from having copies of *The Knoxville News-Sentinel*, whose stories sometimes quoted representatives of both sides in the disputes. *The New York Times* was slow to report on happenings in Harlan. Prior to the 1931 Battle of Evarts, the paper had published only six such news items. Later, in connection with the National Miners Union's attempts to organize workers in the county, the paper printed 119 stories about the ongoing coal war.[22]

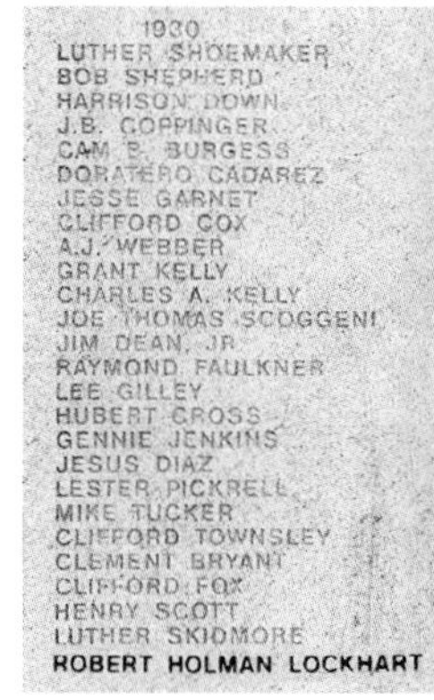

The Harlan County Coal Operators Association

The most consequential event in Harlan's history was the creation of the Harlan County Coal Operators Association. Formed in 1916, the group's membership included almost every major coal company in the county. Over the subsequent decades it came to control local politics and repeatedly defeat the miners' attempts to unionize. As the Association's power grew, it gained control of every aspect of the county's social fabric, from wage rates to policing and the courts. The newspaper, the schools, even the churches, all answered to the local coal operators. And at those few mines whose workers did manage to establish a union, it was typically defeated within a few years.

The county sheriff was the principal instrument of the operators' control.

They say in Harlan County, there are no neutrals there,
You'll either be a union man or a thug for J.H. Blair.
Which side are you on? Which side are you on?
Which side are you on? Which side are you on?

Once Florence Reece's song about J.H. Blair had made its way around the county, the sheriff had no chance of getting reelected. At that point, Theodore Roosevelt Middleton, Harlan's chief of police, stepped up as the reform candidate. He promised to treat union miners equally, to fire all of Blair's deputies, and even to give equal protection to the holiness churches that sometimes allowed union meetings. Middleton teamed up with Morris Saylor, the candidate for county judge, and they took office on Jan. 1, 1934. But no sooner had they been elected than the two men switched sides. Middleton retained all of Blair's deputies, who became even more

Sheriff J.H. Blair. Knoxville News-Sentinel, January 7, 1934.

aggressive toward striking miners. And according to one account, while Middleton was in office, "He greatly increased his personal fortune and acquired five coal mines and an interest in a coal-camp commissary and a leased coal property."[23]

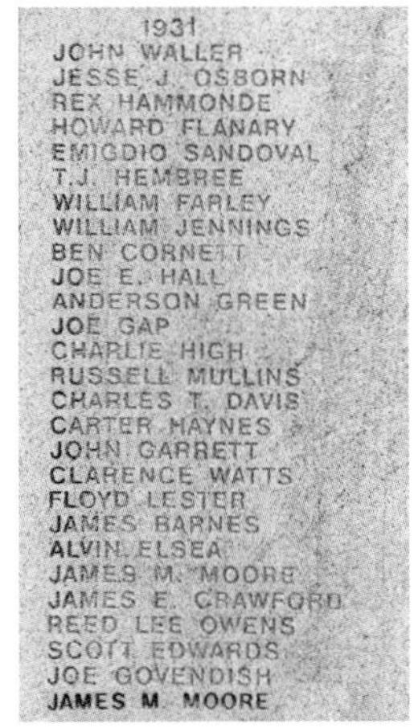

In Kentucky at that time, the county judge had to approve the appointment of sheriff's deputies. In Harlan County, 64 of the 169 deputies had been indicted, and 37 had felony convictions. Most of them were guards hired by the coal companies and stationed at the mines. Only seven or eight deputies were paid by the county and actually worked out of the sheriff's office. Judge Saylor "became a partner with the sheriff in the commissary and coal-land leasing venture and commissioned all the sheriff's deputy appointments."[24] In 1936, testimony before the U.S. Senate's La Follette Committee would show that Sheriff Middleton demanded (and got) kickbacks from his deputies. Each time they were paid, they gave a portion to the sheriff.

The year before, the Denhardt Commission, a state investigatory body, had reported that "in Harlan County there exists a virtual reign of terror, financed in general by a group of coal mine operators in collusion with certain public officials; the victims of this reign of terror are the coal miners.... There is no doubt that Theodore Middleton, sheriff of Harlan County, is in league with the operators and is using many of his deputies to carry out his purposes."[25] The La Follette Committee subsequently heard from dozens of witnesses who confirmed those findings.

CHAPTER 4

THE SCRIP SYSTEM

The British

The history of scrip did not begin in the American coal mines. For many years, British businesses had experimented with ways to pay their workers in something other than cash. Some employers paid only in goods. In the 17th century, for example, if a company made nails, it might pay in nails. Similarly, at the end of the week, lace-makers might find themselves supplied not with money but with lace that they then had to trade or sell in order to buy food.

Such goods were called "truck." Long before there were motor vehicles, the word referred to whatever things a truck might carry: articles of any kind. Often, however, it meant garden produce, a usage that survives in our phrase "truck garden."

"The truck system ... was a pair of related but distinct practices. The first of these was outright compulsion upon employees to accept payment of wages in overvalued commodities, usually groceries, or compulsion to deal with a company store under unfavorable terms.... The second form of the truck system was compulsion to deal with a company store if a worker made an irregular anticipation of his wages, accrued but not yet paid."[26]

Every few years, the injustice of the situation generated another act of Parliament. Over time, this resulted in an almost comical number of such laws which regulated wages in England, Scotland, Wales and Northern Ireland. Thus, there is the Truck Act of 1464 and the Truck Act of 1725, as well as later iterations in 1819, 1831, 1887, 1896 and 1940.[27]

All of those legislative actions sought to put an end to the truck system, but by the time the corporations had finished weakening them, they proved to be ineffective. The Crown seldom enforced the law, and the courts were reluctant to impose meaningful penalties. In all cases the employers lobbied mightily to exempt their respective industries and to make breaking the law as painless as possible for the masters. One act, for example, called for fining violators 5 pounds, which was hardly a deterrent.

After initially relying on bookkeeping to keep the accounts straight and then switching to paper coupons, the corporations started using metal scrip. These coins were specific to the company that had them made. Workers could use them to buy food in specially designated "Tommy shops," which had agreed to accept the scrip and then be repaid by the company. Before long, however, corporations saw the wisdom of running those enterprises themselves, and the first company stores were born.

The oldest piece of scrip in my collection is a halfpenny from the Anglesey Mines in Wales. It features a druid priest with an oak-leaf wreath on one side, and a date of 1788 on the other.

Anglesey Mines had an operation at Parys Mountain where an enormous deposit of copper had been mined since the Bronze Age (3300 to 1200 B.C.). Because the company was copper-rich, it didn't stint when it came to weight. The token had almost a halfpenny's worth of copper in it, so it had actual value; most other scrip could only be exchanged for goods.

The Anglesey halfpenny, issued in 1788.

Workers used this and other Anglesey scrip at the company's own store, but it was widely used by other industries as well and became, in effect, a de facto alternate currency throughout the area. In 1817, England declared the Anglesey scrip to be illegal.

Reducing costs boosts profits, and businesses could not resist using the power that company stores gave them. By increasing prices in the commissaries, companies effectively lowered wages. Workers fought back,

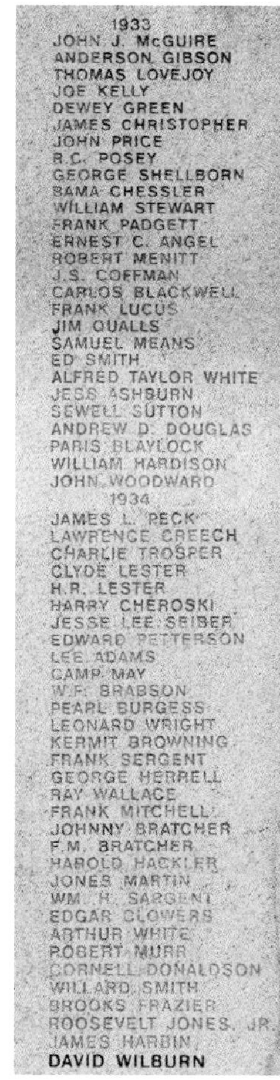

sometimes going on strike or engaging in food riots. When miners looted the truck shops in South Wales in 1816, the Monmouthshire magistrate, J.H. Moggridge, proposed the Truck Act of 1819—which prohibited paying wages in goods.[28]

By 1831, however, employers had found a new way around the law: Don't pay wages in truck. Instead, provide groceries as an advance on wages earned but not yet paid. Thus, in a fine stroke of semantic hairsplitting, the company wasn't paying in goods and so was not violating the law. Workers who could wait until payday would receive cash. But wages were so low that most employees couldn't do that; instead, they were forced to accept overpriced food from the commissary in order to feed their children. A well-paid worker wouldn't need an advance on wages. A hungry one did, and the scheme effectively kept the truck system working (albeit under a different name).

The Americans

American coal companies did not have to navigate the learning curve as the British had. They simply adopted the strategy outright, establishing company stores across the continent.

According to Stuart Brown, scrip was used as early as 1863, when a Pennsylvania state senator named Lowry proposed "An Act to Prevent the Payment of Workmen and Laborers in Orders Upon Store Keepers." Sen. Lowry said that the companies had "coined money out of base metals having a fictitious value but stamped PAYABLE IN STORE GOODS."[29]

The law was passed but the Pennsylvania Supreme Court overturned it, ruling that requiring workers to be paid in lawful money at regular intervals was "an insulting attempt to put the laborer under a legislative tutelage, which is not only degrading to his manhood, but subversive of his rights as a citizen of the United States. He may sell his labor for what he thinks best, whether money or goods, just as his employer may sell his iron or coal."

Apparently, the court wasn't swayed by the Constitution's stipulation that "The Congress shall have power to coin money, regulate the value thereof, and of foreign coin, and fix the standard of weights and measures."[30] The way the court saw it, Congress had the power to coin money—but so did the Godcharles Mining Co. of Milton, Pennsylvania.[31] Other coal companies quoted that decision in their always successful efforts to protect the scrip system.

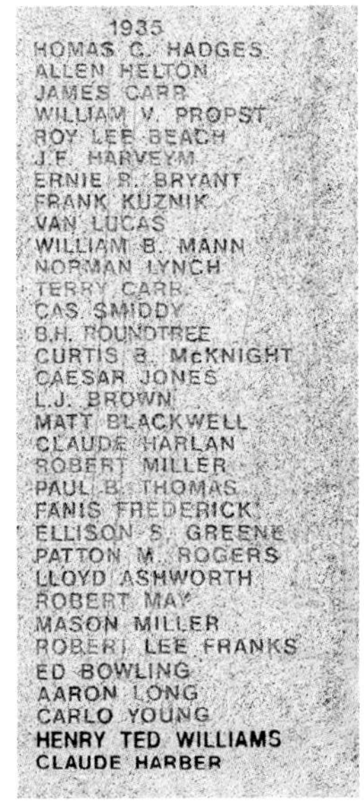

The company store was the only place that one could spend the scrip and prices were higher, often much higher, than other stores nearby.

The companies made the pay period two weeks instead of the usual one week. Companies usually hold back the first payday, so that a miner who was hired on the first of the month was not paid until the end of the month, thus ensuring that he had to use scrip to get by.

The Pennsylvania Anthracite Strike of 1902

Anthracite, a clean-burning, hard coal, is greatly concentrated in a few Pennsylvania counties. It was heavily used in Eastern cities, and a strike in the anthracite fields would disrupt the economy and cause trouble for President Theodore Roosevelt in the 1902 midterm election.

High prices at the company store, short weight at the scales, and unsafe conditions in the mines all contributed to the strikes that plagued the coalfields, but it was the low wages and long hours that finally sparked the 1902 strike. Wages in the anthracite fields were so low that the miners would run out of money to feed their families long before payday came. The operators had anticipated this, of course, so they made scrip available. The miner went to the boss and asked for scrip, and if he had worked enough hours, it was issued and the amount deducted from his pay.

The miners spoke multiple languages and were divided into different groups accordingly, yet they effectively closed the mines for almost six months. They stood united against private police forces, dangerous working conditions, child labor, blacklisting, and short weight.

Gov. William A. Stone dispatched his entire National Guard to the coalfields, and President Roosevelt threatened to send in the army. Former President Grover Cleveland wrote to Roosevelt, saying that the miners should first go back to work and then negotiate a settlement.

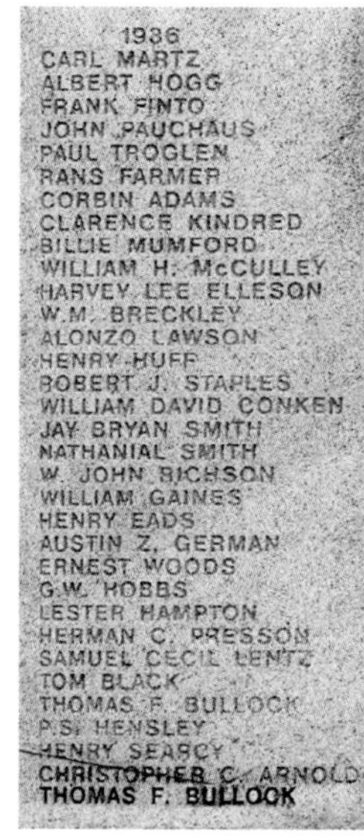

Elihu Root, Roosevelt's secretary of war, had been a well-known corporate lawyer and was a friend of banker J.P. Morgan, who asked Root to come to New York. On Oct. 11, 1902, the two men met for five hours on Morgan's yacht and agreed that a commission would be appointed to arbitrate the dispute. Eventually the miners were forced to settle. They got a 10% wage increase and a nine-hour day (down from the 10-hour days they'd worked before). They didn't get union recognition or an end to the scrip system.[32]

But while the miners did not achieve all their goals, the experience showed workers and employers alike that a successful strike could force meaningful change. Although the strikers weren't immediately able to end child labor, for example, the photographs that Lewis Hine took during that period made a difference in public perception and paved the way: Pennsylvania's *Child Labor Act of 1905* prohibited children younger than 14 from working in the mines.

Breaker Boys, 1911. Lewis Wickes Hine

Pennsylvania prohibited employing children younger than 14 from working in the mines, but these children seem much younger. Maybe the companies are skirting the law by employing the children not in a mine but in a tipple. Note the rod in the older boy's hand.

System Scrip

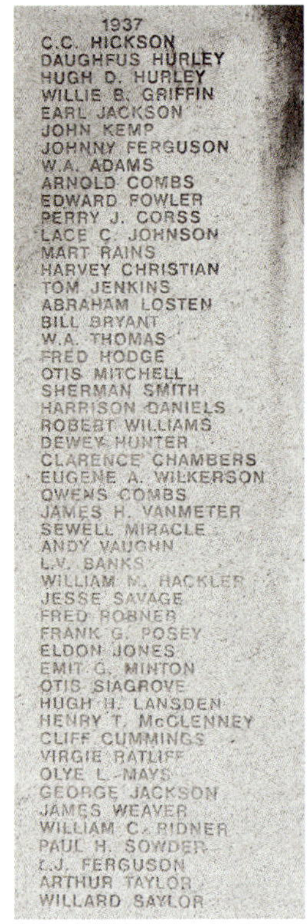

In both countries many of the earliest pieces of scrip were made of paper, which meant that any printer could produce a credible copy. Early scrip coins could easily be counterfeited as well. To counter this problem, "system scrip" was invented. This entailed copyrighting and patenting both the tokens themselves and the special registers that dispensed them. It worked because die sinkers would not want to violate the copyright or patent.

Examples of system scrip.

Three of the system scrip makers were Master Metal Scrip, the Insurance Credit System and Osborne Register Company (Orco).

The Ingle System Co. (later renamed the Insurance Credit System) pioneered the practice in 1908. The cash register had only recently been invented, and both companies used specially modified models to dispense the tokens.

Then in 1920 Wiley Osborne started the Osborne Register Co. (Orco). He had worked as an engineer for Consolidation Coal Company for four years. The company had well over 100 mines in which it used scrip, so Osborne knew the system well.

Scrip from the Consolidation Coal Co., Monongah, West Virginia.

In 1922, he applied for a patent on his scrip register. In the application he wrote:

> My invention relates to trade-check credit machines, for use by concerns in communities where the trade-check credit system is or would be employed. This trade-check credit system is used extensively in coal, ore and other mine offices and commissaries, as well as lumber camps, oil fields and construction camp offices and commissaries... It is customary in such communities to make the intervals of wage payment of longer duration than in the most closely populated centers, for the reason of inconvenient banking facilities and the necessity of carrying large sums of cash over long distances. These intervals of wage payment are usually either monthly or semi-monthly.
>
> In the particular class of wage earners employed by business interests of the character stated in such camps and communities, there will be found many who administer their own personal financial affairs in such a way as to seldom have ready cash available for the purchase of such material and supplies necessary to their subsistence. It has, therefore, been the practice of such companies to make financial advances on workmen's earnings and yet avoid the necessity of handling cash in transactions of this nature.[33]

An Osborne Scrip Register. This one is from Harlan Collieries Co. at Brookside.

An example of a receipt from a scrip register at Stanaford, West Virginia, with a scrip dollar from that location.

A steel die used in a stamping press to stamp the coal scrip tokens from blanks along with the token produced by it. The "A" cutout was added in a later step.

Subsistence wages were clearly the reason miners struggled to survive from one payday to the next, but Osborne neatly shifted the blame by disparaging the workers' financial management skills, leaving one to wonder how it could be that every camp was filled with such spendthrifts. And his claim that longer pay periods made it less dangerous to transport large sums of cash over long distances makes no sense, because doubling the pay period would double the amount of cash that had to be carried.

The Osborne Co. manufactured scrip to order and then the coal companies issued it, using the patented registers, to miners seeking an advance. The scrip clerk set the machine to dispense one, two, three, four or five $1 scrip pieces; the machine produced a printed record for the miner and retained one for the company.

Automating the issuance of scrip was a tremendous timesaver for the coal companies. Work that would have consumed several payroll clerks could then be done quickly. As one of Orco's ads pointed out, in less than an hour a 10-year-old child could issue $600 in scrip to 200 employees.[34]

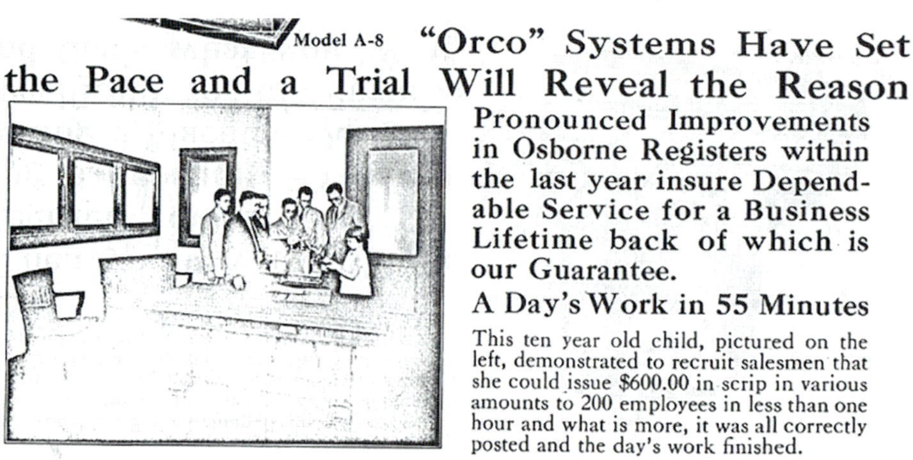

CHAPTER 5

EVARTS

Evarts is an incorporated town, not a coal camp. Many of the camps have disappeared, but Evarts was there before the coalfields were developed, and it still exists today. Miner and author Jim Garland called it "a free town, a town not owned by any company."[35]

In 1949 when I was 4, my family moved from Punkin Center to Evarts, and I grew up there. The photograph shows almost the entire downtown.

There's a diner in the center of the photograph below, underneath the Royal Crown Cola sign. They cooked with coal in that restaurant, and you can see the smoke coming out. Just above the smoke, you can see a slate dump on the hillside. Sometimes my brother and I would go there to collect

Evarts, 1946. Russell Lee

scraps of coal that had been overlooked. (If you're ever cold in coal country, another good place to look is along the railroad tracks. The tipple workers heap up the gondolas, expecting the coal to settle during its journey, but sometimes they don't get it quite right and some falls out. If the gons are parked on a siding, sometimes you can help it fall out.)

Just past the bridge on the right side of the photo is a sharp left turn near where the Battle of Evarts took place in 1931.

Dr. Pierce was the doctor at the Black Mountain coal camp, and on the left of the photograph is Pierce's drugstore. Just after that there's an alley with crossties on cinder blocks along the sides, which was a convenient resting place for the townsmen.

When I was 10 or so, I walked down that alley and came upon a man, old to my eyes, who was telling some young miners a story. Pointing to the mountainside, he said they had burned crosses high above the town, that they had cut the limbs off the trees, tied planks on them to make giant crosses, and then set them aflame. Everyone was scared, he said, describing the sound of one shot after another.

The shock of that part of the story blotted out the rest, and not long after, I climbed that hill. It seemed to me that he had pointed directly at the slate dump. There was no sign of a cross or a fire, and I suppose I didn't expect there to be. I didn't think about the story much, and as I got older I came to believe that he had been mistaken. I never heard another reference to it and just stopped thinking about it.

But years later, when I read historian John Hevener's book *Which Side Are You On?,* I remembered what he had said. After the Battle of Evarts, Hevener wrote, the trial of the miners was set for Monday, April 17, 1931, in Harlan Town, and the union members had planned a rally for that day. But Sheriff J.H. Blair banned all public demonstrations during the trial. On the Friday and Saturday nights before the trial was due to start, "The glare of flaming crosses illuminated the mountains overlooking the county seat, and ominous blooms of exploding dynamite echoed across the valley to call attention to the spectacle."[36]

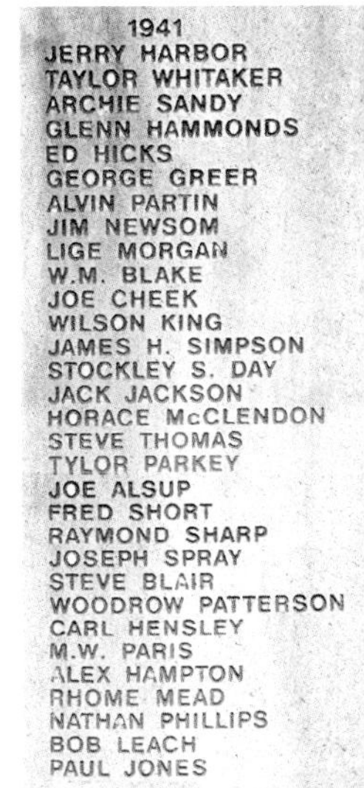

The man in the alley had said "shots," but in the mines, that's what dynamite blasts are called. And he'd been pointing not to these particular hills but, in his mind's eye, to the ones over the town of Harlan. Cross burnings, church burnings, and evictions were all strategies Southern planters used to keep sharecroppers and tenant farmers in line. Now they were being used against miners.

These terror tactics are, rightfully, closely associated with the racist aggression of groups like the Ku Klux Klan. But many people are unaware of their routine use against unions as well. There's a long history of such attacks on textile workers, cigar-makers, and citrus laborers—and far too often they would include a flaming cross.

In the 1950s, Evarts was segregated: The schools were segregated, and so were the neighborhoods. The Roslyn Theatre required Black people to sit upstairs. My mother took us to church regularly and, like everything else in town, her church was segregated too. But one evening we arrived to find six or seven Black people in attendance among the 30 or so white regulars.

A slate dump. This is not part of coal mining—the photograph shows a man looking for usable lumps of coal.

My mother became acquainted with one of the women, Sister Meeks. (In her church, men were "brothers" and women were "sisters.") She came to our house at least twice, and we went to hers a time or two when I was 5 or 6.

I never asked my mother about that, but I never forgot it either. And then I read this:

> It was not uncommon to find, for example, more than one Church of God in the same coal camp or town. This was the case in the commercial town of Evarts. Evarts had two Church of God (Cleveland) churches: one white and one 'colored.'... Members of white and black congregations frequently attended one another's revival services and other special meetings.[37]
>
> *–Carletta A. Bush*

Mystery solved. Not surprisingly, the friendship forged by Sister Meeks and my mother did not survive our town's segregation. But that relatively progressive position on race was matched by the pro-union sentiments of some of the churches, which repeatedly led to trouble with the coal companies.

How did unionism survive in a county where union workers were regularly beaten, imprisoned and killed, and where they were fired and blacklisted by the hundreds? According to Bush, writing in her doctoral dissertation, *Faith, Power, and Conflict,*[38] it was the toehold that the union miners had in the local Holiness churches that kept the unionist fires banked.

In addition to Evarts, Bush writes that by 1931, "The towns of Ages, Harlan, Highsplint and Twila were homes to both churches belonging to the Church of God (Cleveland) and local unions of the United Mine Workers of America."[39]

With the parallel rise of unionism and the Holiness church, several preachers led the union movement at critical times. Churches inside the coal camps were usually built by the coal companies, and they often also paid the minister's salary. Not surprisingly, union-minded miners stayed away from those churches, but they were welcomed at the Holiness and Pentecostal churches that miner/preachers built outside the bounds of the camps. And when ministers allowed union meetings to be held on the premises, the coal operators directed their fury toward both the preachers and their congregations.

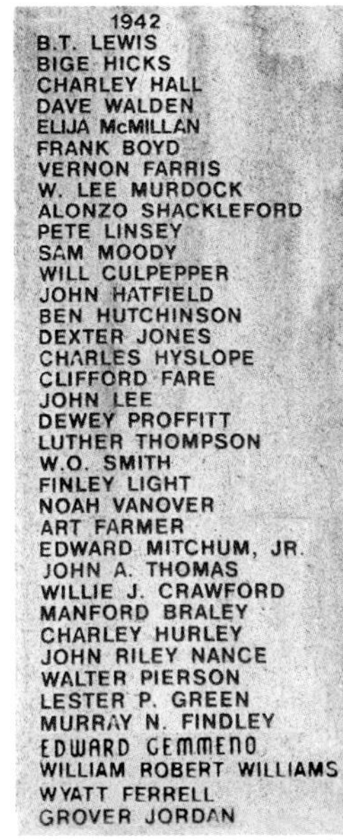

The Strike Wave of 1931

In February of 1931, the mines affiliated with the Harlan County Coal Operators Association announced a 10% wage cut.[40] Times were already hard, with many mines running only three or four days a week. The new cut pushed miners, already hungry, toward literal starvation, and miners across the county went on strike, saying they could either "work and starve" or "strike and starve."

The companies responded by firing and evicting the strikers. In Alva, the Black Star Coal Company fired 60 workers, who then began holding union meetings at the community church. Soon afterward, the church was burned down. Other churches were dynamited.[41]

When the evictions started, many people moved away. If they had kin who could come and retrieve them, they went home and doubled up with whoever would take them in.

Many others, though, had nowhere to go, and no way to get there. Hardly anyone had a car or truck, and very few had a horse or mule. For

Draper commissary, the company store of the East Harlan Coal Co. after a break-in. Widespread starvation led to repeated break-ins of stores in the spring of 1931. (Newspaper Enterprise Association, May 9, 1931)

most, their feet were their sole mode of transportation. And so they walked to Evarts, carrying what they could and leaving the rest.

Early in 1931, the town saw a massive influx of evicted miners. Harlan-Wallins Coal Company in Verda, 3 miles west of Evarts, fired 49 miners and evicted 49 families. Black Mountain Corp. in Kenvir, 3 miles southeast of Evarts, fired 175 miners and evicted 175 families.[42] Within a few weeks, Evarts' population swelled from 1,500 to 5,000.[43]

These families, as well as more from up on Clover Fork, moved to Evarts, and the town opened its doors to them. Sheds were filled, one family to a shed. Then two families to a shed. After that it was stables, garages, attics, basements, crannies. Families doubled up and then tripled up. If you were going to be in a union together, you had to support one another. Nobody was comfortable, and not everyone survived.

But the miners weren't really in a union: They merely hoped and expected that the United Mine Workers would support them. Those hopes proved to be unfounded. Although they formed UMW Local 5355, it was purely aspirational; an organizing local that had no contracts and, therefore, no means of support.

Meanwhile, the children had already started dying of starvation—or, as the official phrase had it, "died of malnutrition-induced disease." Dysentery (also known as "the bloody flux") and pellagra caused most of the deaths. In Harlan County in 1929, 56 children starved to death. In 1930,

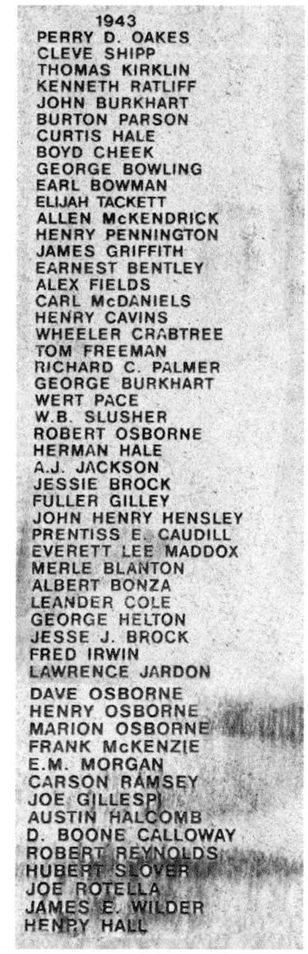

REPORT OF THE

CHILD RELIEF WORK

IN THE

BITUMINOUS COAL FIELDS

BY THE

AMERICAN FRIENDS SERVICE COMMITTEE

SEPTEMBER 1, 1931
AUGUST 31, 1932

HARLAN COUNTY

American Friends Service Committee—District No. 5-A

Anna J. Haines, District Director

No.	Schools	School Enroll-ment	Children on Relief in School	Relief Feeding: Started	Stopped	Number Days Meals Served	Total Number Meals Served	Pre-School Children	Nursing and Expectant Mothers
1	Cawood	224	75	11-12-31	7-15-32	168	8,564	2,493	749
2	Wilsonberger	120	100	11-17-31	7-15-32	157	11,184	4,772	1,709
3	Wallins	555	140	11-23-31	7- 8-32	163	16,926	5,950	
4	White Star	76	60	11-24-31	7- 1-32	158	9,456	5,732	2,275
5	Shields	207	80	12- 3-31	7- 8-32	152	11,257	9,808	1,886
6	Draper	76	76	12-15-31	7- 8-32	149	8,696	1,972	770
7	Elcomb	200	140	12-16-31	7-15-32	138	15,353	2,335	1,330
8	Cumberland	750	250	12-28-31	4-15-32	75	17,686		
9	Black Joe	70	36	12-31-31	7- 8-32	137	4,564	3,596	1,617
10	Evarts	445	220	1-14-32	7- 8-32	124	19,990		
11	Red Bud	58	26	1-25-32	5- 6-32	70	1,820		
12	Shields (colored)	26	26	2-10-32	7- 1-32	101	2,426		
13	Cotes	45	45	2-24-32	6-17-32	83	3,310		
14	Ages	160	100	2-25-32	5-20-32	57	5,983		
15	Kentenia	120	31	3-14-32	7-15-32	90	2,466		
		3,132	1,405				139,681	36,658	10,336

% school children on relief to school enrollment: 44.8%.
Total meals served: 139,681.
Pre-school children receiving rations: 263.
Nursing and expectant mothers receiving rations: 69.
Total rations served to pre-school children, nursing and expectant mothers: 46,994.

91 children died. In 1931, the death toll hit 84. There were 231 fatalities in all; most were infants or toddlers.[44]

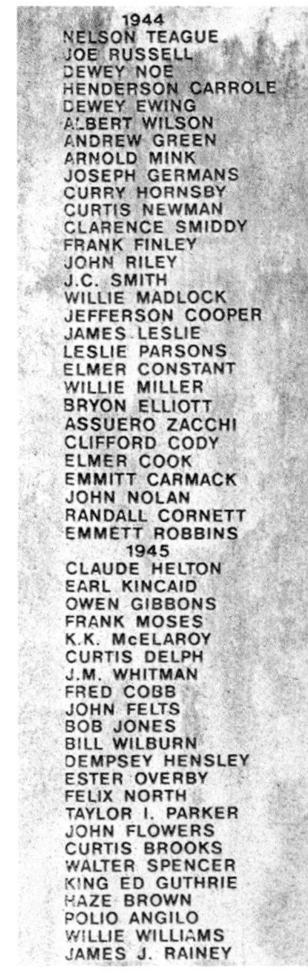

In adjacent Bell County conditions were just as bad, perhaps worse. Aunt Molly Jackson, a midwife, watched many of the babies she'd delivered up on Straight Creek sicken and die. She said, "I talked to the Red Cross lady over in Pineville. I said there's a lot of little children in destitution. Their feet are on the ground..." She said, "We are not responsible for those men out on strike. They should go back to work and work for any price that they will take them on for."

> *No food, no clothes for our children, I'm sure this ain't no lie,*
> *No food, no clothes for our children, I'm sure this ain't no lie,*
> *If we can't git more for our labor, we will starve to death and die...*[45]

In Harlan, there was no government assistance of any kind, and the Red Cross, the only organization that could have helped, refused, maintaining that to feed the children would be to take part in a labor dispute. The Red Cross failed to help across the coalfields, always saying that they could not take sides.As we will see in a later chapter, the National Miner's Union set up kitchens to feed the starving families, but the coal operators shot them up, dynamited others, and in one case killed the men operating the kitchens.

Finally, after promising to feed only the children, not adults, and to refrain from making public pronouncements about the conditions there, the American Friends Service Committee was allowed to come into the county. Starting in September, 1931, they set up fifteen kitchens in Harlan County, mostly in schools, and their report says they fed 1400 children for periods ranging from 2 months to 8 months. They opened several kitchens in Bell County as well.

A similar strike broke out in Wilder, Tennessee, in 1934. According to author J.B. Thompson:

> There was nothing in Wilder but the coal mines, the miserable little shacks the company rented to the miners, the company store and one or two sad, unpainted churches. The company paid the miners in scrip instead of money, so they had to buy their food and other

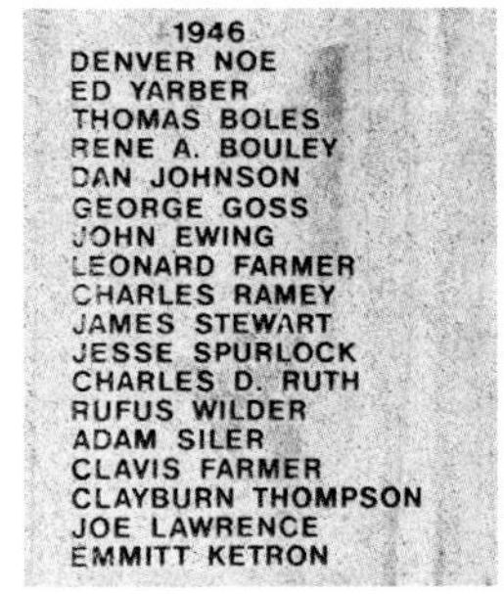

> necessities in the company store, where the prices were much higher than at independent stores. The company made deductions for a bathhouse that didn't exist, for doctor's services which seldom were available, for house rent, etc., etc. The miners worked hard and dangerously but sank deeper and deeper into debt. They didn't have enough to keep their children alive, so finally they went out on strike. They were affiliated with no outside organization; they just had a little union of their own.[46]

The strikers sang a song about conditions there called "Miners' Flux":

They are shooting starving miners here,
And framing men to jail.
They cheat us in the company store,
And cheat us at the scale!
And the bosses spend a million bucks,
On jewels and on silk,
While our children die of bloody flux
Because they have no milk.
They are clubbing men and women here,
Because they ask "more bread."
The bosses' justice orders cops
And thugs to give them lead.[47]

As the Harlan strike spread, the deputies became more and more belligerent. They were in charge of evicting striking miners, and some—including Jim Daniels, the head mine guard at Black Mountain—did it with more gusto than others.

Daniels already had a reputation among the miners. World War I was still fresh in everyone's mind, and Kaiser Wilhelm was the prototype bully, so Daniels was nicknamed "The Kaiser" for his terrorizing tactics. He and a group of other deputized guards drove around with guns sticking out the windows; when they saw pickets, they would bear down on them as if intending to run them over.

These deputies had no training as police officers and, as noted, were more likely to be on the other side of the law. The only reason they were

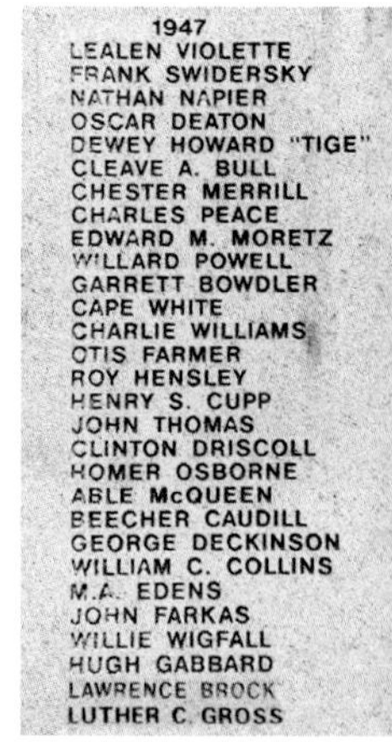

deputies was that having arrest powers made them more useful to the coal operators. But they were rough and tough, and that's what was wanted. No law governed the mine guards' behavior: Instead, they were the law.

In the private deputy system, only a handful of deputies were employed by the sheriff's department. The rest were employed by the mining companies, usually as guards, but also as store clerks and in other jobs.

Jim Garland wrote about taking a Black Mountain miner to the doctor and getting stopped by a mine guard. The man had been burned by the electric cable on the coal-cutting machine he'd been running, but the guard claimed the miner was drunk and wanted to arrest him. After examining the man, the guard finally let them go. According to Garland, "This gun thug was Jim Daniels, one of the men who was killed at Evarts in 1931. He was kicking a Negro man when he got his: Someone shot his head off with a shotgun blast. He was a mean man."[48]

Sociologist Alessandro Portelli interviewed a woman named Charlene Dalton, who talked about her grandmother. "She was married at 12 years old to Jim Daniels and it was an abusive situation, because he was a pretty fast man, you know."[49]

Jesse Pace

On April 17, 1931, a mine guard from Black Mountain named Jesse Pace was called to Evarts, along with several other deputies, to help arrest some union men who were said to have beaten up a nonunion miner.

While making the arrest, Pace spotted a union miner named Bill Burnett walking away. Burnett wasn't one of the miners the deputies had come to arrest, but when he turned away, Deputy Pace shot at him, hitting him three times. Burnett returned fire and killed Pace.[50]

Burnett was promptly arrested. According to the sheriff, the coal operators, and the newspaper,

Miner Jailed For Murder Of Deputy Sheriff

Marks 8th Violent Death This Year in Kentucky Soft Coal Regions

WORKERS TO STRIKE

Final Plans for Walkout Friday Are Drafted at Mass Meeting

Headline in *Louisville Courier-Journal*.

Burnett was guilty of first-degree murder. But in the eyes of the townspeople and the striking miners, he was innocent. (When Burnett's trial came up seven months later in Mount Sterling, Kentucky, far from Harlan County, he was found not guilty, having acted in self-defense.)

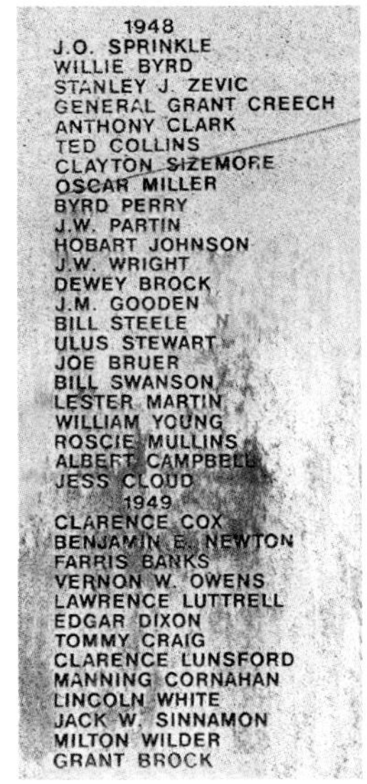

The newspaper headline said "Miner Jailed for Murder of Deputy Sherrif." But the facts and the law, as well as the eventual verdict, warranted a different headline, perhaps "Deputy Killed After Shooting an Innocent Man." The killing generated repeated headlines, however, pushing the narrative that the miners were a murderous bunch and that the deputies were merely trying to maintain order. Because the coal operators controlled *The Harlan Daily Enterprise* and the local courts, their version of these events prevailed right up to the Mt. Sterling court's acquittal of Bill Burnett.

Despite the verdict, the county attorney wouldn't let it rest. After Burnett was found not guilty, he was arrested again and charged with assaulting the other deputy, who was in the line of fire when Burnett killed Pace. And in this trial, Burnett was convicted and served prison time. Thus, he was exonerated for the deputy he killed but convicted for the one he missed!

And even that is not the end of the story. The mine guard's widow applied for compensation, since her husband had been killed as a result of his employment with the Black Mountain Corp. The Workmen's Compensation Board awarded her and her three small children $12 per week for 335 weeks, and the Harlan Circuit Court upheld the award.

Black Mountain appealed the court's decision, however, and Judge Thomas, who heard the case at the Kentucky Court of Appeals, clearly did not understand how things worked in Harlan County. In 1934, the judge ruled that when Pace went to Evarts to carry out an arrest, he was working for the Sheriff's Department, not the company—and therefore Black Mountain was not obliged to pay. (You can read the Court of Appeals opinion at harlanscrip.com, the companion web site to this book.)

Apparently, Thomas didn't know that the companies, not the sheriff, paid the mine guards for their work. The fact that the guards had been deputized by a sheriff controlled by the coal companies was simply a way to ensure that the guards could more efficiently serve their employers' purposes. On the other hand, the Compensation Board knew who employed Pace and so did the Circuit Court, so naturally they found for his widow.

The lawyers on both sides knew this too, regardless of whether they chose to share that information with Judge Thomas. For that matter, it's an open question whether Mrs. Pace's lawyers really worked for her or for Black Mountain.

Four years later, in 1938, 22 coal companies and 24 operators went on trial in federal court in London, Kentucky. C.B. Spicer, who'd been one of Mrs. Pace's attorneys, now worked for the coal companies, and he paid witnesses to testify that union miners, not deputy sheriffs, had killed Bennett Musick, the son of a union organizer. Spicer was subsequently disbarred, but his work for the companies and his willingness to suborn testimony on their behalf calls into question whose interests he was really representing in the Pace case.

In any event, Mrs. Pace wound up with a dead husband and three small children to feed, and Black Mountain never had to compensate them. The Jesse Pace case also foreshadowed what came next: The Battle of Evarts.

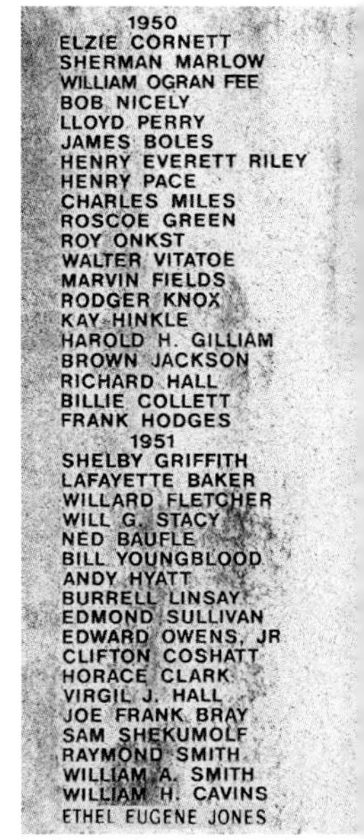

The Number 1 Mine at Lejunior Russell Lee

CHAPTER 6

THE BATTLE OF EVARTS

The Battle of Evarts was a turning point in the coal war in Harlan. The shootout itself changed little, but the operators used it to destroy the union and keep organizers at bay for another seven years.

The striking miners at Black Mountain's Kenvir operation maintained picket lines as they tried to prevent strikebreakers from taking their jobs. And since any potential strikebreakers would have to pass through Evarts to get to the mine, it made sense to have the picket line there, in friendly territory, rather than closer to Black Mountain.

On the morning of Tuesday, May 5, 1931, Sheriff J.H. Blair ordered three carloads of deputies to travel from Black Mountain to Verda to escort a strikebreaker back to the Kenvir mine. As usual, there were two versions of the incident.

The sheriff maintained that those three cars were ambushed by a mob of strikers who hid in the bushes and opened fire, killing three deputies. In returning fire, the deputies managed to kill one miner.

When the case came to trial, the government claimed that the ambush had been planned the night before. According to the prosecutors, some 300 people attending a union meeting at the Roslyn Theatre in Evarts had heard the union president publicly instruct the miners to bring their guns. And three government witnesses—brothers Fred, John and Hugh Lester—testified that the union secretary, William B. Jones, had said, "Shoot to get meat, shoot their God damned heads off." But no witness who had attended the meeting supported what the brothers said.

Nonetheless, the first reports carried on the AP wire (presumably from *The Harlan Daily Enterprise*) said that there were 40 miners at the scene of the shooting. By the time the trial started, the government prosecutors were claiming that a hundred to a hundred and fifty miners had been present. These claims were mainly intended for the newspapers though; the prosecution witnesses themselves testified that there were just twelve to fourteen pickets when the shooting started.

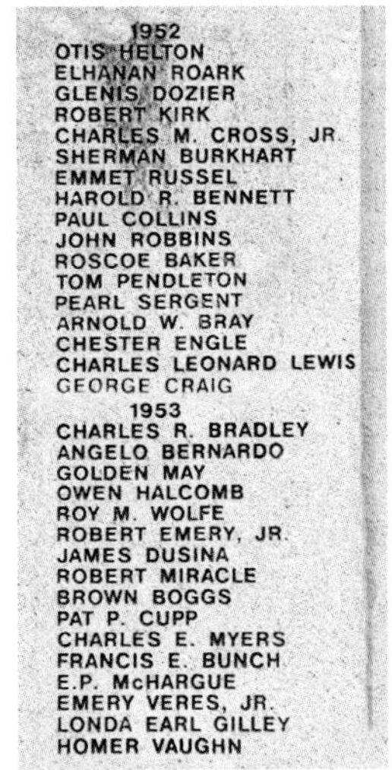

The government's version was that the pickets had lain in wait in a roadside thicket and opened fire on the three cars carrying 10 deputies. A thousand shots were fired, and the battle lasted 30 minutes or more. Three deputies were killed, two more were wounded, and the rest escaped in two of the cars. The dead deputies were Jim Daniels, also known as "The Kaiser," Howard Jones and Otto Lee. One union miner, Carl Richmond, was also killed.

The county judge called a grand jury into session and procured indictments against 43 union members and supporters for murder. An additional 100 miners were charged with "banding and confederating."

Among those charged with murder were William Hightower, the president of Local 5355, the aspirational chapter the miners had formed in hopes of gaining UMW support; William B. Jones, the local union's secretary; Evarts Police Chief Asa Cusick; Assistant Chief Al Benson; merchant Joe Cawood; and UMW District President William Turnblazer. In fact, none of these men were present at the shootout. Hightower was actually in Harlan talking to Sheriff Blair at the time of the battle, and Turnblazer wasn't even in Harlan County.

Cawood had lost to Blair in the sheriff's race in 1929. In Evarts he was widely known for being pro-union and for helping displaced miners. He housed some who'd been evicted, and he donated generously to others in need. As a merchant, he hoped to do away with the stranglehold the company store had over the miners' pay. What's more, Cawood was expected to run again in 1933, so charges against him were convenient for his political opponents. Chief Cusick was also a prominent political figure who might be expected to run for office in the next election.

The Defense

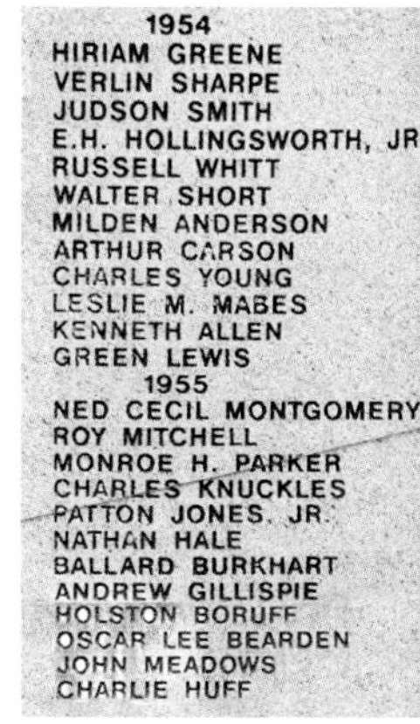

The Lester brothers, the prosecution's star witnesses, had previously been indicted for the poisoning death of their employee, Lonnie Prince, in order to obtain a $20,000 insurance payout. They were also charged in connection with the shootout. Yet, after they agreed to testify for the Commonwealth in the Evarts case, all charges were dropped. Some defense witnesses, however, said the Lesters hadn't attended the union meeting; others testified that they'd seen the brothers elsewhere at that time.

And those were not the only problems with the government's case.

How could the ambush have been planned the night before, when even the deputies themselves did not yet know they would be sent to escort a strikebreaker? And if they had somehow known about the planned attack, why didn't the brothers warn the sheriff ahead of time? Furthermore, why would experienced union men plan a crime in public when they knew the coal operators always posted spies at those meetings?

The defense also pointed out that the pickets could not have known the deputies would be coming from Black Mountain. Earlier that day, the company had dispatched a truck to move the belongings of the strikebreaking miner the deputies were supposed to be escorting. The pickets in Evarts had seen the truck when it passed through town on its way to Verda, so they knew it would be coming back through Evarts on the return journey.

That means the pickets would have been facing toward Verda, not Black Mountain. And when the deputies' cars came up behind them, defense witnesses said the deputies started shooting even before their vehicles came to a stop, and that when they did, Jim Daniels got out an automatic rifle and opened fire.

Besides, if armed miners had been lying in wait for the deputies as the prosecution claimed, how could any of them have escaped? As it was, seven deputies and two of the cars had been able to continue on their way toward Verda. It's hard to see how

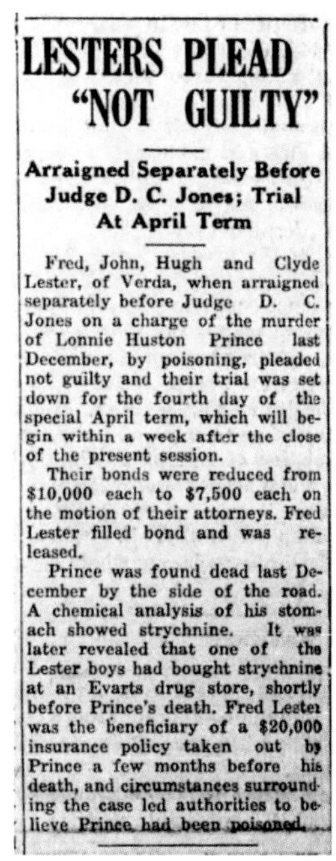

LESTERS PLEAD "NOT GUILTY"

Arraigned Separately Before Judge D. C. Jones; Trial At April Term

Fred, John, Hugh and Clyde Lester, of Verda, when arraigned separately before Judge D. C. Jones on a charge of the murder of Lonnie Huston Prince last December, by poisoning, pleaded not guilty and their trial was set down for the fourth day of the special April term, which will begin within a week after the close of the present session.

Their bonds were reduced from $10,000 each to $7,500 each on the motion of their attorneys. Fred Lester filled bond and was released.

Prince was found dead last December by the side of the road. A chemical analysis of his stomach showed strychnine. It was later revealed that one of the Lester boys had bought strychnine at an Evarts drug store, shortly before Prince's death. Fred Lester was the beneficiary of a $20,000 insurance policy taken out by Prince a few months before his death, and circumstances surrounding the case led authorities to believe Prince had been poisoned.

Harlan Daily Enterprise, March 31, 1931

that could happen if there had indeed been 100 armed men, or even 40, ambushing them. Wouldn't the fusillade of 1,000 shots have killed them all and disabled the three cars?

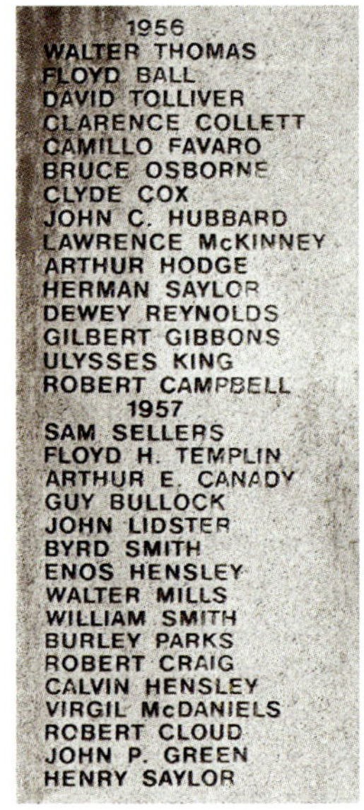

The actual death toll is far more consistent with the defense's theory than the prosecution's. After all, terrorizing pickets was what the deputies did. What was new was the level of aggression: Rolling up on the pickets from behind and starting to shoot from inside their cars. Perhaps they did not expect the miners to shoot back, because in the past, they typically had not. It was only 18 days since Bill Burnett had shot Jesse Pace, and that was the first time a union miner had killed a deputy.

Usually, all the shooting in these clashes was done by the deputies, and they used their weapons to intimidate, not to kill. They would brandish their machine guns out their car windows, sometimes firing in the miners' direction, but not really at them. It would be completely in keeping with their past behavior to fire at a crowd of strikers, and their mediocre aim makes sense if they were shooting from moving vehicles.

When the deputies gunned down Carl Richmond, however, the miners fired back, killing three deputies.

The New York Times gave an account in one of its stories that supported the miners' version. According to reporter Louis Stark, the shooting began when the cars came to a stop and Deputy Daniels got out, set up a machine gun, pointed it toward the crowd of union pickets at the side of the road, and shot and killed a union miner. It was at this point that some in the crowd returned fire, killing the three deputies.[51]

We will never know exactly what happened—it's been almost 100 years, and there are many differing accounts of the battle—but what is clear is that major parts of the prosecution's case were fiction.

© Olha Bosenko

The Aftermath

On May 7, over 300 National Guard troops arrived at the Evarts train depot, armed with machine guns. They brought battle tanks into the county as well, but those were never used. Over the following days they disarmed the miners, broke up the picket lines, dispersed crowds, and escorted the strikers who were willing to return to work back to the mines.

And yet that didn't end the strike. Not only did it continue, it expanded. Historian John Hevener writes, "On the day of the battle, 1,800 miners were out; six days later, 5,800 Harlan miners were on strike, leaving only 913 at work."[52]

Then Bell County followed suit. "On May 16, at a UMW rally in Pineville, 800 Bell County miners vowed, almost to a man, to mine no more coal until the Harlan guards were removed."[53]

For the next several years, the strike, the shootings in Evarts, and the trial of the men accused of murder generated headlines in papers across the country. "Bloody Harlan" was now a refrain.

It wasn't until much later, after the federal La Follette Committee hearings and the 1938 trial of the coal operators, that it become apparent that the deputies were the murderous ones. In the meantime, there was only a tangle of wildly differing accounts.

National Guard troops atop a commissary. Note the framework for wet weather tarps.
Courtesy of Ehren Bowling

The Murder Trials

Law school 101: When the facts are on your side, pound the facts. When the law is on your side, pound the law. When neither the facts nor the law is on your side, pound the table. The prosecutors had lost the Jesse Pace/ William Burnett murder case to the facts and the law, so when the Evarts case came up, they pounded the table and painted the miners as puppets of world communism.

During Jones' trial, prosecution attorney W.C. Hamilton used his closing argument to make numerous allegations that had not been supported by the testimony. He claimed that Jones, the secretary of the UMW local in Evarts, was linked to the Industrial Workers of the World and to the National Miners Union, a communist-led alternative to the UMW. During recruiting marches, Hamilton maintained, Jones "carried an American flag in his hand but the red flag of the IWW was in his heart." And if Jones were freed, the prosecutor predicted, "There will be a celebration of Reds."[54]

Two tanks were dispatched along with National Guard troops in May, 1931.
Herndon Evans, University of Kentucky Special Collections.

Up until that point, the only union active in Harlan had been the decidedly anti-communist UMW. By artfully misstating the timeline, the prosecutors redbaited these miners. Rather than prove the defendants' guilt, the prosecutor "proved" that they held objectionable political opinions. In fact, it was only after the United Mine Workers retreated when confronted by the National Guard that the National Miners Union sent organizers into the county.

Nonetheless, Hightower, Jones and six other miners were sentenced to life in prison for murder. Seven others were convicted of manslaughter. Four were given four-year sentences, and three received three-year terms. Charges against the rest were dropped, but the convictions crippled the union movement by removing its most seasoned leaders, and while Cusick and Cawood didn't go to prison, their political careers were effectively ended.

Nonetheless, the workers' response—greatly expanding the strike despite the brute display of force—was unprecedented. It also expressed the miners' belief that the deputies had struck first and that the miners who were arrested had merely been defending themselves, just as Bill Burnett had done.

National Guard troops on top of Bardo commissary. Courtesy of Ehren Bowling.

In 1935, the 12 jurors who had convicted Jones petitioned the governor to set him free. The next year, several others—including Dolly Daniels, the slain deputy's widow—asked that Jones be pardoned. This woman, who presumably knew Jim Daniels as well as anyone, believed that all those convicted were innocent.

Cop killers are hunted down and often killed by police. They are widely denounced, and when they come to trial, they frequently get the death penalty. If anyone is likely to die in prison while serving a life sentence, it's someone who kills a law enforcement officer. And yet, a mere four years after their trials, four of the eight strikers who'd been so sentenced were pardoned by the governor, and the rest were pardoned a few years later. In 1935, Gov. Ruby Laffoon pardoned Hightower, William Hudson, Gaines Eubanks and Elzie Phillips; and in 1941, acting Gov. Rodes K. Myers pardoned Jones, Benson, Chester Poore and Jim Reynolds.[55]

Those governors weren't pro-union in any way and, in fact, had repeatedly called out the National Guard against the strikers. But they knew the state's witnesses were untrustworthy, and they believed that justice had not been served.

From the coal operators' point of view, however, the shootings presented an opportunity that should not go to waste. To them, both the April killing of Deputy Pace and the deaths in the Battle of Evarts were murders. They used their control of the sheriff, the county judge, and *The Harlan Daily Enterprise* to turn the trial into a broad attack on unionism.

The Battle of Evarts, or at least the version of it that the operators pushed in the media and the courts, ended the union movement in Harlan County for several years.

The Killings at Crummies Creek

The "Battle of Evarts" was called that only because that description suited the mine operators. Three dead on one side and one on the other, however tragic for those men and their loved ones, doesn't usually qualify as a battle. But the bombast helped the operators gain sympathy for their side, at least for the time being.

On the morning of April 2, 1941, another shootout also left four dead. This time, however, all of them were union men. They'd been picketing a mine at Mary Helen that was not yet organized. Deciding to take a break, the pickets piled into three cars, drove up to the company store at Crummies Creek to buy refreshments, parked, and got out.

Survivors speculated that the guards at Mary Helen must have told the Crummies guards that the pickets were coming, because they unleased volleys from three directions. One machine gun had been set up on the mountain behind the commissary, another on the mountain across the road, and a third weapon, either a machine gun or a Browning Automatic Rifle, in the gable of the commissary.

When the shooting started, the miners retreated to a line of coal gondolas. Some of them returned fire, though they had only pistols. When the shooting stopped and the ambulances came, three miners were dead; another would expire in Harlan's hospital soon after.[56]

Just as at Evarts, four were dead, but this time it was not called a battle.

The Battle of Blair Mountain

A far more deadly confrontation had taken place in Logan County, West Virginia, over a period of several days in August, 1921. Around 10,000 coal miners faced off against some 3,000 heavily armed members of the West Virginia National Guard and employees of the Baldwin-Felts Detective Agency. The National Guard killed between 50 and 100 miners. In the fighting 20 members of the National Guard were killed, and three U.S. Army airmen died when their plane crashed after a reconnaissance mission.

Unlike the later "Battle of Evarts," the Blair Mountain affair was an actual battle—or, rather, a series of battles. The largest armed labor revolt in American history, it featured speeches by Mother Jones, aerial surveillance by the Army, and poisonous bombs dropped from the coal operators' private airplanes.

At issue was the United Mine Workers' attempts to organize in Mingo and Logan counties, West Virginia; the operators hired the Baldwin-Felts agency to help break the strike.[57]

SEPTEMBER 3, 1921. TWO CENTS In Greater New York | THREE CENTS Within 200 Miles | FOUR CENTS Elsewhere

FIGHTING CONTINUES IN MOUNTAINS AS FEDERAL TROOPS REACH MINGO; PLANES REPORTED BOMBING MINERS

AVIATORS AID IN DEFENSE

Logan Official Hears They Scattered Raiders With Bombs

HEAVY FIRING IS UNABATED

Take Eighteen Miners Prisoner, but Casualty Estimate of Fifty Is Unconfirmed.

FIGHTERS ACCUSE UNIONS

State's Forces Report Evidence of Mine Workers and Reds Engineering the Invasion.

Special to The New York Times.
LOGAN, W. Va., Sept. 2.—With word received that Federal troops are at the

Governor of West Virginia Issues Proclamation Placing All State Officials Under Army Control

CHARLESTON, W. Va., Sept. 2.—Governor E. F. Morgan of West Virginia today issued a proclamation to all State and county officers, civil and military, and deputies, assistants and subordinates, ordering them to co-operate with the United States troops and to obey the direction of the officer commanding the troops or his properly designated representative. The proclamation reads:

To all State and County Officers, Civil and Military, and Deputies, Assistants and Subordinates:

Whereas, United States troops have, at my request, been ordered to this State for the purpose of quelling an insurrection, the peace officers of this State are ordered to co-operate with the United States troops to the end that there may be unity of action.

The peace officers of this State will obey the direction of the officer commanding the United States troops, or his properly designated representative.

DECLARES STATE BROKE ITS PLEDGE

Miners' Leader Asserts New Outbreak Followed Killings by Authorities After Dispersal.

WASHINGTON DELAYS MARTIAL LAW ORDER

Administration Hopes to Avert Extreme Step, Believing the Troops Are Sufficient.

SOLDIERS ARRIVE IN AREA

Bandholtz in Charleston Prepares Campaign to Quell Disorder

FIRST TRAIN TO ST. ALBANS

Others, Including Those From Camp Dix, Are Expected in Zone This Morning.

COMMANDER IS OPTIMISTIC

Thinks Mobs Will Disperse—Word From Miners Is That They Will Obey U. S. Troops.

New York Times, September 3, 1921

CHAPTER 7

THE NATIONAL MINERS UNION

The Battle of Evarts triggered the departure of the United Mine Workers and the arrival of the National Miners Union. The UMW was in retreat everywhere. Between mine closings and layoffs, dues revenue had shrunk to a fraction of what it had been, leaving the union without enough money to provide relief for its current members. New organizing was out of the question.

After the National Guard came into the county with their tanks and machine guns, the UMW abandoned the field. The union held a meeting or two, but it had no solutions to offer and no funds to support striking miners. It had already given up in eastern Ohio, western Pennsylvania and east Tennessee, and now it withdrew from eastern Kentucky as well. The United Mine Workers had long since kicked the leftists out of the union and even bragged about it. Organizer George Titler wrote, "All members of the UMWA are proud of the fact that the coal miners' union was the first in the nation to prohibit membership to Communist Party members."[58] They seemed to think that if they actually had no communists or socialists in their ranks, the companies would stop redbaiting them. That didn't work. The Pineville Sun's editor, Herndon Evans, called those proud anti-Communists "reckless agitators," "radicals" and "violence-prone." The Harlan Daily Enterprise regularly decried "foreign radicals" attempting to destroy the country.

In 1928, some of the left-leaning miners and organizers who were kicked out of the UMW had formed a new group, the National Miners Union. Now, with the UMW in retreat, the new union organized a convention in Pittsburg and invited Kentucky miners, including some from Bell

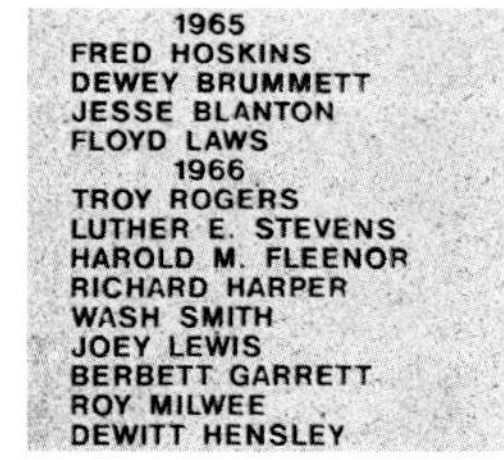

and Harlan counties. Miners who attended asked the NMU to come into those counties, where they said that large numbers of workers were ready to organize. The NMU promised to help and sent several organizers into eastern Kentucky.[59]

Historian John Hevener has called the miners' movement in 1931 the "Union of the Damned," and for good reason. The Great Depression had cut demand for coal to the point that many mines were running only two or three days a week, and some had closed down completely. Between 1929 and 1932, annual coal production in Harlan County dropped by more than half, from over 14 million tons to less than 7 million. For the miners, what had been subsistence wages at 50 or 60 hours a week became starvation wages at 20 or 30.[60]

Meanwhile, the local union leaders were in prison, masses of miners had been arrested, a thousand were blacklisted, and hundreds had been evicted from the camps. Nonetheless, the miners increasingly chose to strike: It was the only tool they had. It may sound foolish to do that when nobody wants your work in the first place, but the only other option was sitting back and doing nothing while you watched your loved ones starve.

In 1931, thousands of workers struck without an organizer in sight. They struck without the backing of a national union, and knowing full well that the company could, and often did, evict workers from company housing. That's desperation, and that's what happened in Harlan County.

Politically, the miners' cause in Harlan and Bell counties was about as hopeless a case as could be found. The operators controlled every lever of power, from the sheriff's office and the courts to the state government. And the local press, at least, took its cues and marching orders from the mine owners, though the national news outlets were considerably better and often reported both sides of the story.

But if the miners had no money to support their own efforts, the NMU wasn't much better off. Stretched thin, it depended on donations, not regular union dues, to maintain itself. Striking when the operators don't need your labor is a losing tactic, but what else could they do?

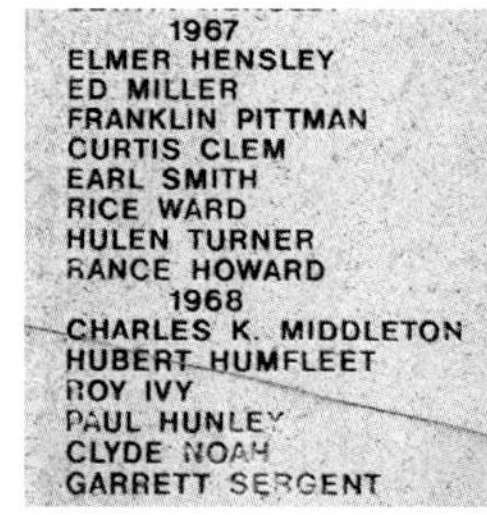

The UMW was correct in its assessment that, under the circumstances, there was little chance of obtaining a contract and therefore, from a trade union point of view, little sense in striking. But the NMU was an altogether different animal. The upstart union focused on supporting the miners however it could while considering the impact even limited achievements might have on the broader labor struggle.

The miners responded enthusiastically to the new union's efforts. Within weeks of the first two NMU organizers entering the county, 10 new locals were established.[61] Radical newspapers were widely available, and NMU organizers were eager to share their conviction that, for working people, socialism was a better deal than capitalism. Equally important, they were ready to roll up their sleeves and do whatever could be done to help.

Food was among the most pressing needs, and in July 1931 the NMU opened seven soup kitchens in Harlan County and one in neighboring Bell. From the very beginning, however, they were under attack. On Aug. 11, deputies arrested two brothers who were staffing one of the facilities. That same morning, the kitchen in Evarts was dynamited. Later that month, the deputies arrested Debs Moreland, who was operating the Pansy kitchen. They held him for a month, but when he got out he reopened it. This time the deputies kidnapped him, beat him and forced him to leave the county.[62]

On Aug. 30, Deputy Lee Fleenor shone his headlights on the Clovertown soup kitchen. When the three men inside came out, he shot and killed two of them and seriously wounded the third. Arrested much later, Fleenor was acquitted. By October, the only kitchen still operating was the one at Arjay, in Bell County.[63]

The other thrust of the new union's efforts was publicity. If the public truly understood what was happening—the brutality, the hunger and the repression of civil rights—maybe something would be done. To that end, the NMU organizers and other progressives wrote articles, gave speeches and staged concerts. Left-leaning writers covered the trials of the union men from the Battle of Evarts, and the NMU raised funds for their defense. Ironically, the men they were helping were the leaders of the rival UMW.

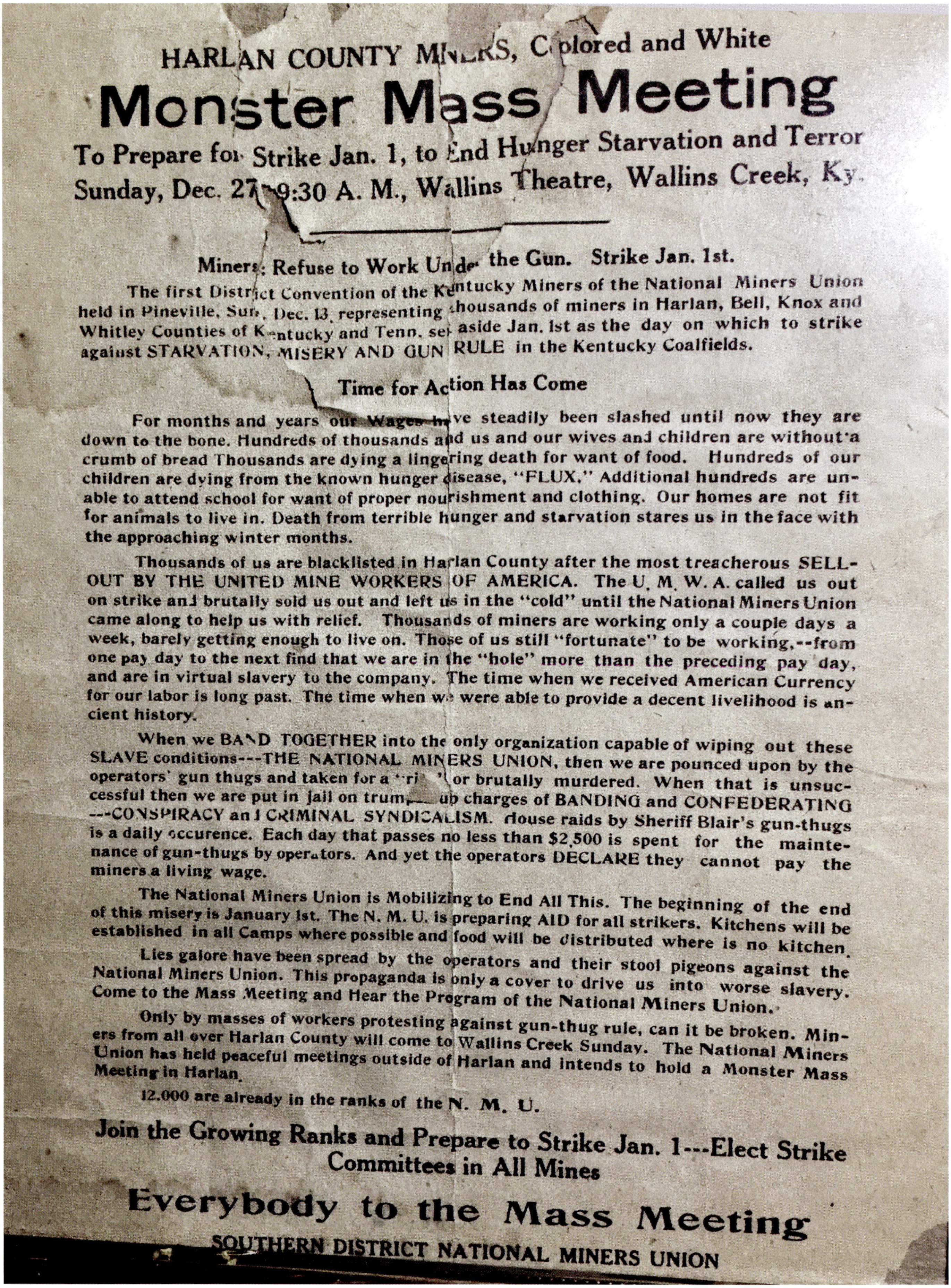

HARLAN COUNTY MINERS, Colored and White

Monster Mass Meeting

To Prepare for Strike Jan. 1, to End Hunger Starvation and Terror
Sunday, Dec. 27—9:30 A. M., Wallins Theatre, Wallins Creek, Ky.

Miners: Refuse to Work Under the Gun. Strike Jan. 1st.

The first District Convention of the Kentucky Miners of the National Miners Union held in Pineville, Sun., Dec. 13, representing thousands of miners in Harlan, Bell, Knox and Whitley Counties of Kentucky and Tenn. set aside Jan. 1st as the day on which to strike against STARVATION, MISERY AND GUN RULE in the Kentucky Coalfields.

Time for Action Has Come

For months and years our Wages have steadily been slashed until now they are down to the bone. Hundreds of thousands and us and our wives and children are without a crumb of bread Thousands are dying a lingering death for want of food. Hundreds of our children are dying from the known hunger disease, "FLUX." Additional hundreds are unable to attend school for want of proper nourishment and clothing. Our homes are not fit for animals to live in. Death from terrible hunger and starvation stares us in the face with the approaching winter months.

Thousands of us are blacklisted in Harlan County after the most treacherous SELL-OUT BY THE UNITED MINE WORKERS OF AMERICA. The U. M. W. A. called us out on strike and brutally sold us out and left us in the "cold" until the National Miners Union came along to help us with relief. Thousands of miners are working only a couple days a week, barely getting enough to live on. Those of us still "fortunate" to be working,--from one pay day to the next find that we are in the "hole" more than the preceding pay day, and are in virtual slavery to the company. The time when we received American Currency for our labor is long past. The time when we were able to provide a decent livelihood is ancient history.

When we BAND TOGETHER into the only organization capable of wiping out these SLAVE conditions---THE NATIONAL MINERS UNION, then we are pounced upon by the operators' gun thugs and taken for a "ri[illegible]" or brutally murdered. When that is unsuccessful then we are put in jail on trumped up charges of BANDING and CONFEDERATING ---CONSPIRACY and CRIMINAL SYNDICALISM. House raids by Sheriff Blair's gun-thugs is a daily occurence. Each day that passes no less than $2,500 is spent for the maintenance of gun-thugs by operators. And yet the operators DECLARE they cannot pay the miners a living wage.

The National Miners Union is Mobilizing to End All This. The beginning of the end of this misery is January 1st. The N. M. U. is preparing AID for all strikers. Kitchens will be established in all Camps where possible and food will be distributed where is no kitchen.

Lies galore have been spread by the operators and their stool pigeons against the National Miners Union. This propaganda is only a cover to drive us into worse slavery. Come to the Mass Meeting and Hear the Program of the National Miners Union.

Only by masses of workers protesting against gun-thug rule, can it be broken. Miners from all over Harlan County will come to Wallins Creek Sunday. The National Miners Union has held peaceful meetings outside of Harlan and intends to hold a Monster Mass Meeting in Harlan.

12,000 are already in the ranks of the N. M. U.

Join the Growing Ranks and Prepare to Strike Jan. 1---Elect Strike Committees in All Mines

Everybody to the Mass Meeting

SOUTHERN DISTRICT NATIONAL MINERS UNION

Flyer from the National Miners Union, December, 1931. Courtesy of Burley Williams

Which Side Are You On?

In a coal camp in Molus, on Harlan's far western edge, Sam Reece worked for the Harlan-Wallins Coal Co. An active supporter of the NMU, he had heard that the sheriff's deputies were looking for him, so he made himself scarce. It wasn't long before the deputies came looking for Sam and any union literature they might find, terrorizing his family. In a later interview, Florence Reece described what happened:

John P. Saylor was the company store for Harlan-Wallin Coal Co.

"Sheriff J.H. Blair and his men came to our house in search of Sam—that's my husband—he was one of the union leaders. I was home alone with our seven children. They ransacked the whole house and then kept watch outside, waiting to shoot Sam down when he came back. But he didn't come home that night. Afterward I tore a sheet from a calendar on the wall and wrote the words to "*Which Side Are You On?*" to an old Baptist hymn, 'Lay the Lily Low':

> *They say in Harlan County,*
> *There are no neutrals there.*
> *You'll either be a union man,*
> *Or a thug for J.H. Blair.*
> *Which side are you on?*
> *Which side are you on?*

"My songs always goes to the underdog—to the worker," she told the interviewer. "I'm one of them and I feel like I've got to be with them."[64]

The song spread across the coalfields and then to other industries. By the 1940s, the entire union movement knew it: Pete Seeger, the Weavers and the Almanac Singers (whose founding members included both Seeger and Woody Guthrie) all recorded it. Later on, a diverse array of artists including Joan Baez, Arlo Guthrie, the Dropkick Murphys, Ani DiFranco, Elvis Costello, Billy Bragg, Natalie Merchant and Rage Against the Machine followed suit, adapting the lyrics to suit their particular cause and times. Many singers retained that first verse in homage to the song's origins.

In 1962 Reece's song found new life during the Civil Rights Movement. The Freedom Singers, a group formed by the Student Nonviolent Coordinating Committee (SNCC, pronounced Snick), rewrote the lyrics as follows:

Come all you Negro people, lift up your voice and sing,
Will you join the Ku Klux Klan or Martin Luther King?
Which side are you on?
Which side are you on?[65]

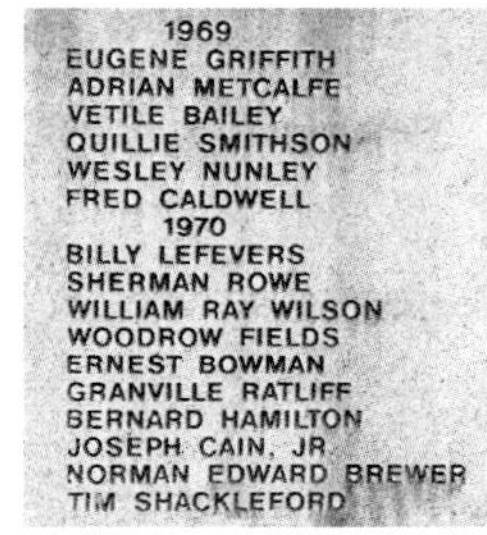

Some who heard the song and didn't know about its roots assumed that it was purely a product of the Civil Rights Movement—and in a broader sense, it was. Because the right to assemble, to freely associate, to vote—all those are civil rights that were denied to the mostly white miners in Harlan County.

In 1965, Bob Dylan crammed over 100 cultural references into Desolation Row, and line 50 reads, "Everybody's shouting, Which side are you on?!" In 2012, Ani DiFranco released ¿Which Side Are You On?, with every song written by DiFranco except for the title track by Florence Reece, sung by DiFranco, and with a banjo introduction by Pete Seeger.

Folk singers told the story of American workers in language they could understand, using tunes they already knew from church and from juke joints. Songs about the struggles were popular on picket lines and, as a result of the NMU's efforts, in concerts in big cities. This was particularly true in New York City, where large numbers of workers attended.

It took a few years for "Which Side Are You On?" to migrate from Molus, Kentucky, to New York, but it did. Other miners' songs made the move almost immediately.

In November of 1931, acclaimed novelist Theodor Dreiser organized a special committee to visit Harlan's coal mines and investigate allegations of crime and abuse. That month, group members attended a union meeting held at the Arjay Baptist Church soup kitchen in Bell County. As Jim Garland wrote, "My sister Aunt Molly Jackson sang a song she had just recently made up; she called it 'The Hungry Ragged Blues.' The committee was so impressed with the song that they invited her to come back to New York City with them. She did and became a successful fundraiser for the miners' strike relief."[66]

Garland and his sister Sarah Ogan Gunning later joined Jackson, and all three became fixtures in the New York folk music scene. They appeared and recorded with Woody Guthrie, Cisco Houston, Ramblin' Jack Elliott, Burl Ives and others.[67]

Meanwhile, back in eastern Kentucky, the attacks continued. On Dec. 31, 1931, while Garland was speaking to a crowd of 200 striking miners at Kettle Island in Bell County, company officials burned a cross on the hilltop above the meeting place.[68]

Journalists who came to report on the starvation and violence were attacked as well. Bruce Crawford, the editor of *Crawford's Weekly* in nearby Norton, Virginia, was shot and wounded when he visited Harlan, as was a reporter for the Federated Press. *The Knoxville News-Sentinel*, a mainstream paper that insisted on reporting both sides of labor issues, was banned in several coal camps.[69]

One of the most popular and personable of the NMU organizers was Harry Simms, a 19-year-old member of the Young Communist League. On Feb. 10, 1932, he and another man were walking along the railroad tracks out of Harlan County into Bell when they were approached by a mine guard at Kentucky Jellico, a Brush Creek mine owned by Bryan Whitfield. The guard demanded that they give him the leaflets they were carrying and then abruptly opened fire, shooting Simms in the abdomen. He died the next day in the Barbourville hospital.[70] Jim Garland's *The Ballad of Harry Simms* became part of the canon in folk circles.

By the spring of 1932, the arrests and killings had taken their toll, and the last of the NMU organizers left the area. They had no contracts or wage increases to show for their efforts, but the NMU had made an indelible impression on the rest of the country. Thanks to the upstart union, the left-leaning press kept the focus on conditions in the coal fields, and specifically in Harlan. The country's major newspapers and magazines began to take a look for themselves and found the story irresistible. Their continued reporting led to the creation of the Commonwealth of Kentucky's Denhardt Commission, which placed the blame for the lawbreaking squarely on the operators. The report was all the more damning because its author, Henry H. Denhardt, was a retired Army brigadier general and the adjutant general of the Kentucky National Guard.[71] If the man charged with breaking up the miners' strikes in Kentucky faulted the operators, what more could be said?

Plenty, actually. Spurred by the reporting in *The New York Times* and the *Chicago Tribune* as well as *Time* and *Life* magazines, Congress eventually had to act. In 1936 the La Follette Committee, a Senate body charged with investigating violations of free speech and labor rights, spent several months focusing on illegal activities in Harlan County. Sworn witness after sworn witness testified to the killings, beatings, arrests, church bombings and cross burnings that were the hallmarks of a full-fledged Southern terror campaign.

And though the coal operators liked to deride books like the 1932 volume *Harlan Miners Speak*[72] as biased in favor of the union, the story those publications told was no different from the accounts to be found in the national press and the records of the Federal Bureau of Investigation. The operators were beating, arresting and killing union miners in total violation of the law, and no amount of political bias could change that.

According to author Thomas N. Bethell, "The NMU encouraged the miners' wives to participate in the strike by organizing auxiliaries—something the UMW had never done—and its publicists did a remarkably effective job of calling conditions in the coal fields to the attention of the public at large. The mine wars of the mountains were largely a matter of local concern until the NMU arrived; within a few months, magazine and newspaper readers

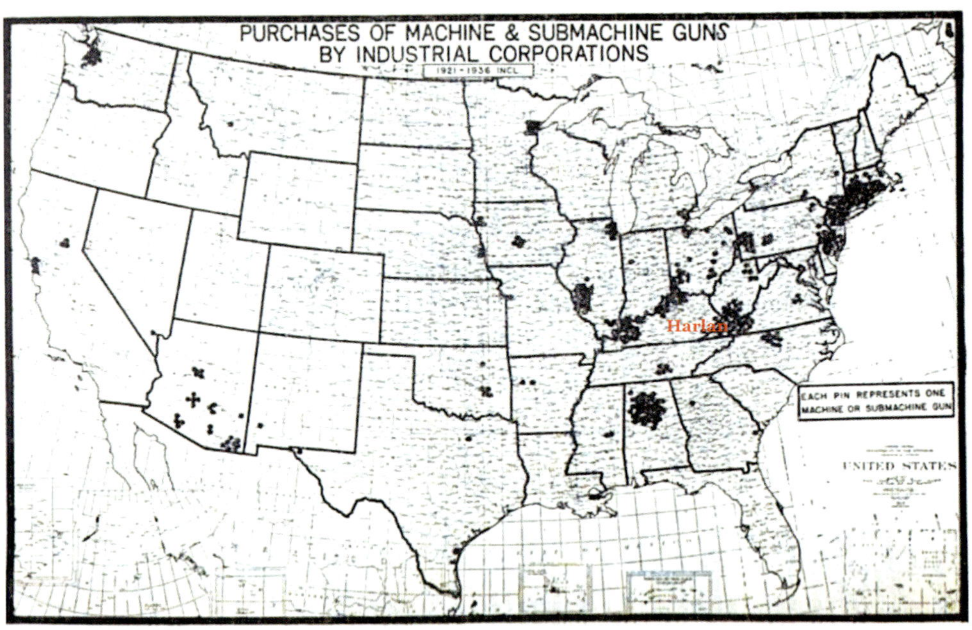

The La Follette Committee mapped corporations' purchases of machine guns from 1921 to 1936. In addition to the large concentrations on the East Coast and Midwest, there's a concentration in the eastern Kentucky-West Virginia area and another in Alabama, centered around coal-producing Walker and Jefferson counties. Note that these guns were not held by the sheriff's departments or National Guard, but by the coal companies.

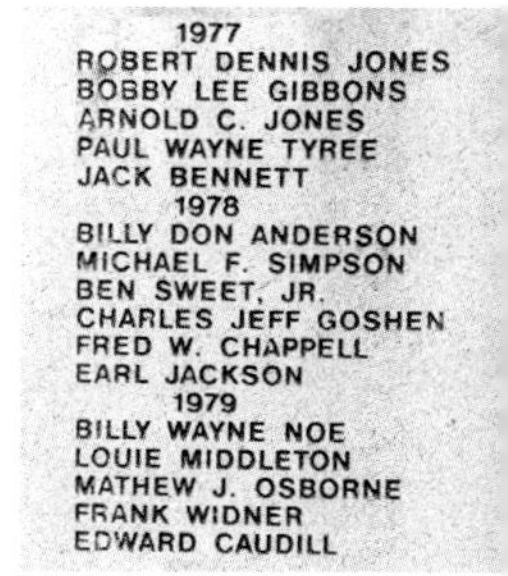

from Massachusetts to California knew about 'bloody Harlan,' and even if the battlefield dispatches sometimes were distorted by revolutionary rhetoric, the stark facts were gripping enough."[73]

The La Follette Committee's findings left the Roosevelt administration with little choice but to investigate, and as we will see, the FBI quickly found ample evidence to charge the operators.

The La Follette committee was focused on the violations of federal labor law, and on the beatings, false arrests, and murders that operators used against the miners. But at one point the committee turned to the commissary–the company store.

According to the Louisville Courier-Journal (April 16, 1937):

> "...one of the high points in Middleton's testimony was when he said that a mercantile company which sells supplies to miners for 'company scrip' is controlled by his wife, the wife of County Judge Morris Saylor, the wife of Pearl Basham, a coal operator, and one Bill Basham.
>
> "Saying that he, himself, had sold the stock to his wife, the high Sheriff–as Chairman La Follette referred to him–said that the $2500 investment had netted a return of $2400 a year."

After he became sheriff, Middleton acquired the Green Silver Coal Corp. Pearl Bassham was an officer in the Harlan-Wallins Coal Corp. and in the Harlan County Coal Operators Association.

When the committee asked him about the Berger Supply Company, Pearl Bassham, said that his wife owned a 25% interest and "receives annual dividends of 1701 per cent on her investment."

The commissary was where the swindle happened, where the labor of the miners was converted into corn meal and beans at almost unbelievable markups. I once tried to calculate the interest rate that miners were paying to use their earnings just a few days early, but gave up when the numbers were so high they seemed impossible. But thanks to the La Follette committee, we have two of the principals, Sheriff Theodore Middleton and coal operator Pearl Bassham, themselves testifying to those markups. Perhaps their testimony explains why the coal companies felt the need to build over 100 new stores in a small mountain county.

The New York Times

SATURDAY, APRIL 17, 1937

THREAT TO WITNESS STIRS COAL INQUIRY

Harlan County Man's Charge Against a Mining Official Is Weighed by La Follette

SHERIFF'S RECORD CITED

Of His 163 Deputies, 'Best Men' He Could Pick, 16 Are Ex-Convicts, 34 Have Faced Indictment

Special to THE NEW YORK TIMES.

WASHINGTON, April 16.—R. C. Tackett, elderly Kentuckian, who told the Senate Civil Liberties Committee of his participation in attempted dynamiting of a Harlan County union organizer, today charged that Ted Creech, a mine superintendent, had threatened him with a jail sentence in conversation at the door of the Senate hearing room.

Creech denied the charge before the committee later, but it will be the subject of a week-end study by Chairman La Follette in an effort to determine whether the committee should formally accuse the superintendent of perjury or intimidation.

The incident followed a day of testimony in which witnesses told of the "lawlessness" of Harlan County deputy sheriffs who, they said, were employed by the mine owners to block unionization.

Creech took the stand and denied their accusation, and while he was testifying Tackett was observed to be trying to get the attention of Chairman La Follette. The chairman permitted him to testify.

"I saw Ted Creech at the entrance to this room after the noon recess," said Tackett. "He told me I had caused the Harlan operators plenty of trouble and he was going to get me back to Harlan County and send me away to jail for ten years."

Marshal Confirms Charges

Tackett, who was awaiting trial in Bell County on a disorderly conduct charge when the Senate hearing started, is spending the period of the hearings in the District of Columbia jail through an arrangement the committee made with county authorities.

He attends the hearings in custody of Deputy Marshal Robert L. Bonham, who confirmed on the stand the testimony of his prisoner.

When the chairman recalled Creech, he stated that the only conversation he had with Tackett consisted of a statement by Tackett that "he had come up here and got drunk and didn't know what he had told the committee."

Sheriff Theodore R. Middleton of Harlan County, who told the committee that in picking deputies "I gets the best men I can," was confronted by official records which showed that of the 163 deputies now on his staff, fourteen have been convicted of crimes of violence under State laws, two had served time for Federal offenses and thirty-four had local records of indictments for crimes of violence.

Relatives on Sheriff's Staff

With regard to Slemp Middleton, brother of the Sheriff, who served as a deputy at various times, the Harlan Circuit Court judge said in a decision that he was "regarded as one of the most dangerous men in Harlan County."

Concerning John Middleton, a first cousin of the Sheriff, who also served as deputy, the court granted a motion for transfer of his trial for willful murder to another county.

This, it was said, was "because it is personally known to the judge that for several years past there has been more crime in Harlan County than in any county in the State of Kentucky, that there has been almost a total disregard of the law and of the life and liberty of the people, and there now exist more than 800 Commonwealth cases on the dockets of the Harlan Circuit Court, many of the charges being against the Middleton family, which is one of the largest families in Harlan County, and a great deal of intimidation of witnesses has taken place in this country, so local jurymen are afraid to do their duty."

Union Head Tells of Beatings

William Turnblazer, president of the United Mine Workers of America for District 19, which includes Harlan County, said it was so difficult for union representatives to operate in the county, owing to "beatings, killings and ambushings from the mountainsides," that even the Bituminous Coal Labor Board under the NRA, when considering Harlan County cases, would meet in neighboring Bell County.

He said that while the NRA agreements were in effect the mine operators "chiseled" on rates and would not obey rulings of the Labor Board.

The Rev. Carl E. Vogel, former Methodist minister at Harlan, told of beatings he saw deputy sheriffs administer to miners, and testified that his campaign with former County Attorney Elmon Middleton to clean up "the collusion between the mine operators and the Sheriff's office" ended in the murder of Middleton.

William M. Clontz, former representative of the U. M. W., related that at one time his dog discovered several sticks of dynamite under his boy's bed and carried the explosives, some percussion caps and a burning fuse outside the house.

"A few days later my dog disappeared and I haven't seen him since," he added.

Lawrence Howard, 27-year-old non-union miner, told of seeing a car run over his dog a few minutes after ten high powered rifle shots had been fired into the Clontz home, less than a hundred yards from his own house.

Out of the car stepped Ben Unthank, the official of the mine owners' association, who has been missing since the Senate hearings started, and Deputy Sheriffs George Lee and Frank White, the witness testified. They had come, he said, from the direction of the shooting.

Howard also told of being offered $100 by Unthank and Lee to do the very shooting job which he described in connection with the killing of his dog.

Reference was made several times to a retainer of $100 a month paid by the Harlan-Wallins Coal Corporation to Daniel Boone Smith, Harlan prosecuting attorney. Pearl Bassham, vice president and general manager of the coal concern, made the first reference to the fee.

Later Mr. Vogel said he told the prosecutor he thought it "didn't appear to be in good faith for a prosecutor to receive a fee from a coal operator."

On July 3, 1932, Clarence Middleton shot and killed a deputy constable named Bill Randolph. Middleton was a store clerk at Three Point Coal Corp. and one of Sheriff J.H. Blair's deputies. According to witnesses, themselves deputies, someone shot and killed Jim Jones and wounded Bill Randolph. When Middleton heard the shots and came over to the scene, he saw that Randolph had been wounded. Middleton pulled out a gun and killed him. He then fled the scene.

He was later arrested, charged with murder and released on bail. When he came to trial five months later, he was immediately found not guilty.

At that time in Harlan County, those who did not pay property taxes were not allowed to serve on juries. Since most mines required miners to rent company housing as a condition of employment, the miners, as renters, were excluded. Most grand juries were made up of merchants, farmers, and coal company officials.[74] But for quick trials, the prosecutor usually sent a deputy to go out onto the courthouse grounds and bring back whomever he could locate. If they voted the way the prosecutor wanted, they were paid a dollar each. If they did not, they were not paid. The sheriff and court authorities routinely allowed perjured testimony, indeed, they often procured it.

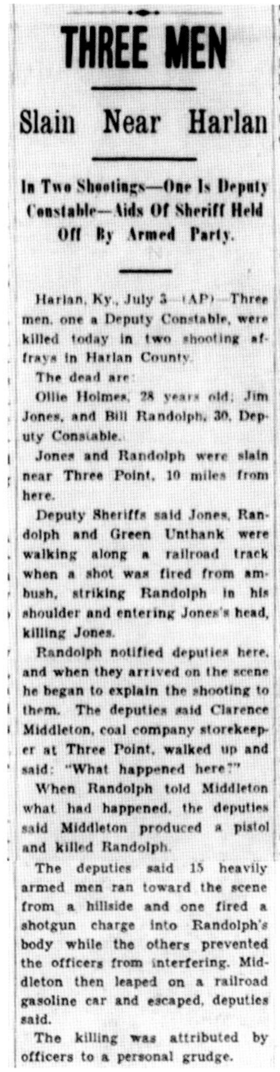

THREE MEN

Slain Near Harlan

In Two Shootings—One Is Deputy Constable—Aids Of Sheriff Held Off By Armed Party.

Harlan, Ky., July 3—(AP)—Three men, one a Deputy Constable, were killed today in two shooting affrays in Harlan County.

The dead are:

Ollie Holmes, 28 years old; Jim Jones, and Bill Randolph, 30, Deputy Constable.

Jones and Randolph were slain near Three Point, 10 miles from here.

Deputy Sheriffs said Jones, Randolph and Green Unthank were walking along a railroad track when a shot was fired from ambush, striking Randolph in his shoulder and entering Jones's head, killing Jones.

Randolph notified deputies here, and when they arrived on the scene he began to explain the shooting to them. The deputies said Clarence Middleton, coal company storekeeper at Three Point, walked up and said: "What happened here?"

When Randolph told Middleton what had happened, the deputies said Middleton produced a pistol and killed Randolph.

The deputies said 15 heavily armed men ran toward the scene from a hillside and one fired a shotgun charge into Randolph's body while the others prevented the officers from interfering. Middleton then leaped on a railroad gasoline car and escaped, deputies said.

The killing was attributed by officers to a personal grudge.

The Cincinnati Enquirer, July 4, 1932

This was the justice system that acquitted Clarence Middleton. His brother, Theodore Middleton, was at that time the Chief of Police of the town of Harlan. Note that Clarence kept his job at Three Point Coal Corporation after this killing, and stayed on as deputy sheriff. Killing a wounded man was not disqualifying for either job.

Deputies who had the power of the sheriff's office but were paid by individual coal companies were a major factor in keeping the union out of Harlan County. At the system's height, in 1937, Sheriff Middleton had 163 deputies on active duty, only three of whom were paid from public funds."[75] The private deputy system was finally abolished in 1938, eight years after Pennsylvania and three years after West Virginia.[76]

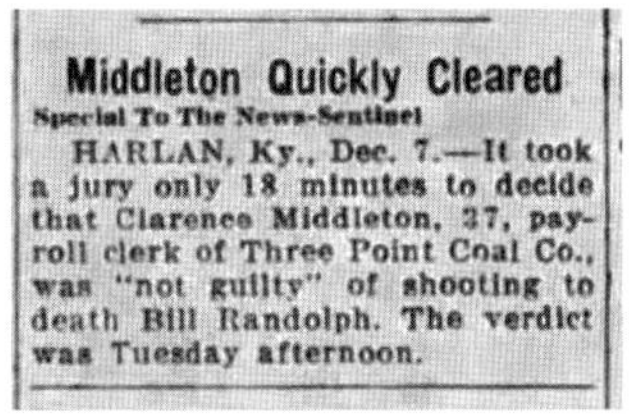

Middleton Quickly Cleared
Special To The News-Sentinel
HARLAN, Ky., Dec. 7.—It took a jury only 18 minutes to decide that Clarence Middleton, 37, payroll clerk of Three Point Coal Co., was "not guilty" of shooting to death Bill Randolph. The verdict was Tuesday afternoon.

Knoxville News-Sentinel

In 1935, Clarence Middleton was still working at Three Point Coal and still a deputy sheriff. By that time, his brother Theodore had been elected Sheriff. Clarence ordered two 357 Magnums from Smith & Wesson. These guns were developed to handle the new 357 Magnum cartridge. Each had a special registration number and so were marketed as Registered Magnums. Only 5500 were produced, and in the gun world they are regarded as one of the best handguns ever made. In 1935, when they were made, they cost $39.00 each.

These guns are now valuable as collectors' items, and collector David Bowling, Sr. bought them for $20,000 each. He bought the first of them at an auction in Oregon, and then back home in Tennessee, he found the second one in the possession of the grandson of Middleton's business partner. (Their business was making moonshine.)

Bowling says, "These guns had been separated for 85 years, 2500 miles apart. When the 76-year-old grandson called me about the mate, I was overwhelmed. I told him I gave $20,000 for the first gun and I would give him $20,000 for his. They are back together and the only handguns in the world with a factory letter that reads: They are to shoot man and not targets."[77]

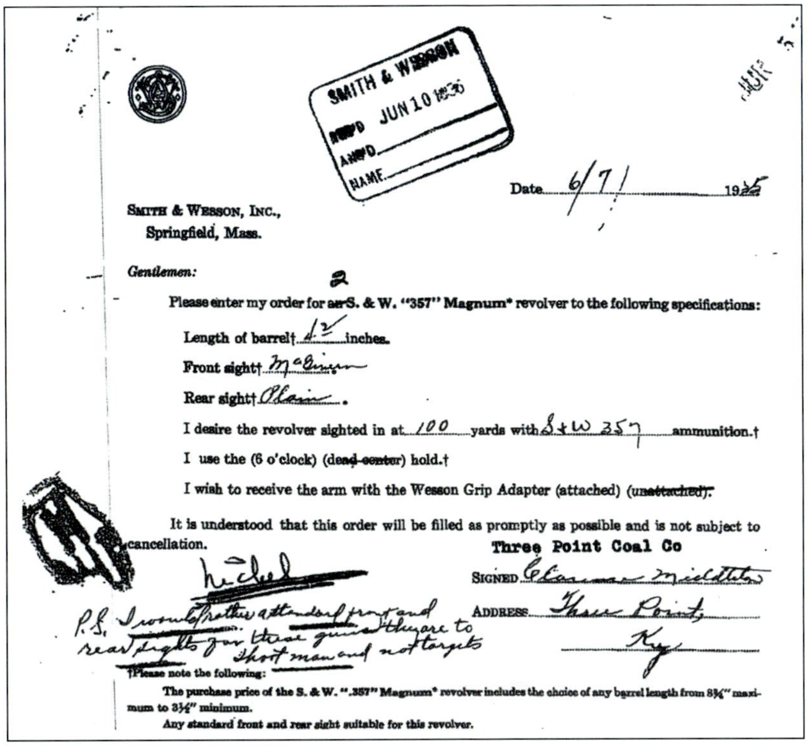

SMITH & WESSON
RECD JUN 10 1935
ANSD.
NAME.

Date 6/7/ 1935

SMITH & WESSON, INC.,
Springfield, Mass.

Gentlemen:

Please enter my order for ~~an~~ 2 S. & W. "357" Magnum* revolver to the following specifications:

Length of barrel† 4 1/2 inches.

Front sight† McGivern

Rear sight† Plain.

I desire the revolver sighted in at 100 yards with S+W 357 ammunition.†

I use the (6 o'clock) (~~dead center~~) hold.†

I wish to receive the arm with the Wesson Grip Adapter (attached) (~~unattached~~).

It is understood that this order will be filled as promptly as possible and is not subject to cancellation.

Three Point Coal Co

SIGNED Clarence Middleton

ADDRESS Three Point, Ky

nickel

P.S. I would rather a standard front and rear sights for these guns. They are to shoot man and not targets

†Please note the following:

The purchase price of the S. & W. ".357" Magnum* revolver includes the choice of any barrel length from 8¾" maximum to 3½" minimum.

Any standard front and rear sight suitable for this revolver.

Deputy Clarence Middleton's order for two Registered Magnums. The note in Clarence Middleton's handwriting reads, "P. S. I would rather a standard front and rear sights for these guns. They are to shoot man and not targets." David Bowling, Sr.

Two Smith & Wesson Registered Magnums purchased by Deputy Clarence Middleton in 1935. David Bowling, Sr.

Witness Intimidation

Mine superintendent Ted Creech stood in the doorway of the Senate Civil Liberties hearing and told a witness that "he was going to get me back to Harlan County and send me away to jail for ten years." The witness, R.C. Tackett, told the Senate committee what was said. Creech denied it, but a U.S. Marshall heard the conversation and confirmed it to the committee. Creech was immediately arrested and charged with intimidating a witness.

"Ted Creech, Harlan County, Ky. coal operator, photographed on the witness stand of the La Follette Civil Liberties Committee hearing in Washington April 20th just prior to his arrest."
– ACME News Photos, Knoxville, Cincinnati, March 20, 1937

CHAPTER 8

THE COAL OPERATORS ON TRIAL

Indictment

If you had 3 cents on Sept. 28, 1937, you could buy a copy of *The Louisville Courier-Journal* with the headline, "Harlan Coal Firms, Individuals Indicted by U.S. Grand Jury." A subhead read, "Conspiracy Is Charged in True Bill." The government charged them all with conspiring to deprive Harlan County miners of rights guaranteed by the National Labor Relations Act of 1935.

The story named 47 indicted individuals, including Sheriff Theodore Middleton and R.C. Tway, the head of the Harlan County Coal Operators Association.

Twenty-two coal companies were indicted:

Bardo Coal Mining Co.
Berger Coal Mining Co.
Black Mountain Corp.
Black Star Coal Co.
Blue Diamond Coal Co.
Clover Splint Coal Co.
Clover Fork Coal Co.
Cornett-Lewis Coal Co.
Creech Coal Co.
Crummies Creek Coal Co.
Harlan Central Coal Co.
Harlan Collieries Co.
Harlan Fuel Co.
Harlan-Wallins Coal Corp.
High Splint Coal Co.
Kentucky Cardinal Coal Corp.
Mahan-Ellison Coal Corp.
Mary Helen Coal Co.
R.C. Tway Co.
Southern Harlan Coal Co.
Southern Mining Co.
Three Point Coal Corp. [78]

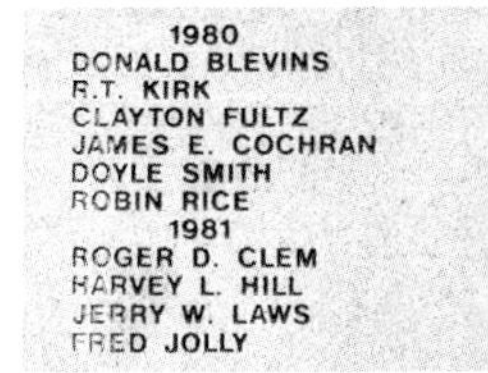

The indictment and subsequent trial generated headlines across the country, and cemented the county in the public's mind as "Bloody Harlan." For weeks on end, news story after news story would tell of yet another atrocity, yet another infraction of the law.

The La Follette Committee hearings had exposed so much wrongdoing that the Roosevelt administration was compelled to act. At the urging of UMW President John L. Lewis and Senator Robert La Follette, Attorney General Homer Cummings ordered 20 FBI agents into Harlan in May, 1937. It took just one month to conclude their investigation, which led to the indictment at Frankfort, Kentucky.[79]

The trial began on May 16, 1938, in London, Kentucky. Every major newspaper sent reporters, and witness after witness proceeded to describe unlawful firings, evictions, beatings and murders. Shaken by the FBI showing up to question him, George Ward, the secretary of the Harlan County Coal Operators Association, admitted to the agent that he had destroyed

69 Harlan Coal Firms, Individuals Indicted By U. S. Grand Jury

Among Harlan County Men Indicted...

Sheriff Theodore Middleton — *Pearl Bassham*

Conspiracy Is Charged In True Bill

By C. W. BAILEY.
The Courier-Journal Frankfort Bureau.

Frankfort, Ky., Sept. 27.—Sixty-nine companies and individuals were indicted by a Federal grand jury here today on charges of conspiracy to deprive employes of rights guaranteed by the National Labor Relations Act. All sixty-nine were accused in one blanket indictment.

The indictment was the culmination of testimony given by coal operators, union organizers and individuals before the La Follette Senate Civil Liberties Committee at Washington last spring. A large number of the individuals appeared before the grand jury here today.

Provides Heavy Penalty.

Louisville Courier-Journal, September 28, 1937

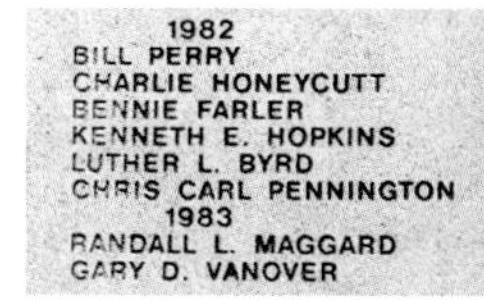

the organization's papers in anticipation of the federal investigation.[80] Others, including Chief Deputy Ben Unthank, could not be found until the proceedings had concluded.

The trial lasted 11 weeks, and by the time it was over, there seemed to be little doubt about the outcome. On the first ballot, however, the jury voted 11-1 for conviction—and that lone holdout was steadfast.

As John Hevener put it,

> "The government's case was lost from the moment jury selection was completed. On the first day of the trial, one juror vowed to others that he 'would rot before he would send a man to the penitentiary to help John L. Lewis, the United Mine Workers or the CIO.'"[81]

The tally remained at 11-1 for conviction until arguments erupted among the jurors that completely transformed the situation. When the dust had settled, five were now voting to convict all the defendants, three for blanket acquittal, and four to acquit some and convict others. The judge declared a mistrial, and the government requested a retrial.[82]

The initial round had cost the operators over $1 million, and they were not eager to do it all over again. The government, however, was willing to cut a deal: If the companies agreed to forgo their most blatant union-busting tactics, and abide by the results of union elections, there would be no new trial. In some cases, the operators set up what were known as "company unions"—employee organizations that looked like unions, but in fact did very little for the miners. They were not legal, but if they could maintain the appearance of independence from the operators, these entities could skirt the law.

Nonetheless, after years of working without union protection, Harlan miners now had some chance of organizing and improving their lives. Eventually many of the mines were organized under the UMW and, for a time, conditions improved.

Throughout World War II, work in the mines was plentiful and paid better than before, but after the war ended, mechanization in the mines soon led to widespread layoffs. The great decline had begun. Harlan County's population plummeted, and as Hevener put it, "The mass exodus to Cincinnati, Cleveland, Chicago, Dayton and Detroit proceeded too slowly to avert widespread unemployment and poverty."[83]

Harlan, Ky,. May 16, 1939 Associated Press Wire Photo

PICKET AND MINE WORKER TANGLE
A tense situation prevailed for a few moments at a coal mine at nearby Totz today when a picket (right) and a worker (left) threatened to engage in a fight. Note the worker reaching into his shirt.

CHAPTER 9

EXPLOSIONS IN THE HARLAN SEAM

The Zero Mine Explosion

The Harlan Fuel Co., owned by the Guthrie family of Knoxville, Tennessee, operated six numbered mines at Yancey: Zero, 1, 2, 3, 4 and 5. At 8:30 a.m. on Dec. 9, 1932, the Zero mine exploded, killing 23 miners; 14 others survived. Flames from the explosion traveled a half-mile through the mine.

Among the dead were six brothers: Henry, Calvin, Garrett, Esaw, Campbell and Thomas Massingale. They had come from Tazewell, Tennessee, with their wives and children and taken work together to protect each other. Now their parents had to come to Harlan County to identify their boys' bodies, one by one.

About an hour and a half after the explosion, Charles Guthrie, the superintendent of the Harlan Fuel Co., notified James F. Bryson about the blast. Bryson, the director of safety for the Harlan County Coal Operators Association, arrived at the site at 11:40, accompanied by the Kentucky district mine inspector, Roy Gonia. The operators thus had their man on the scene straightaway. It was 4 1/2 hours before the federal Bureau of Mines was informed.

After a mining accident, rescue is the first priority, and after that, the recovery of bodies. Whoever is on the scene or can get there does that work. Rather than keeping a rescue-and-recovery team at each mine, the association kept a single crew and its equipment at a centralized location, from which they could be dispatched as needed.

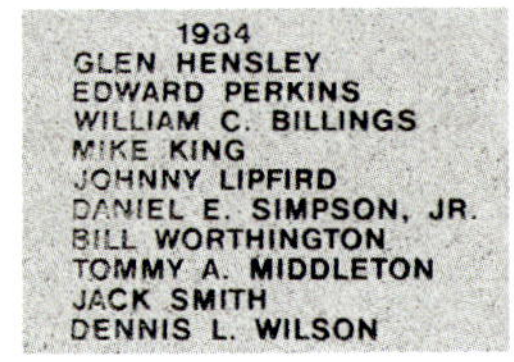

There is nothing improper about company officials or the Harlan County Coal Operators Association being involved; indeed, it is their duty. But it should be left to state and federal authorities to investigate the cause of an accident. The operators' well-known opposition to safety measures in the mines, and their inherent conflict of interest, should have disqualified them from collecting evidence about the cause of the Zero explosion.

By the time the rescue crew arrived at the mine, any hope of rescue had been ruled out; recovery of the bodies began at 2:50 p.m. After they'd been removed from the mine, state and federal inspectors, accompanied by Guthrie and Bryson, went to work to determine the cause of the blast.

Mines blow up when either methane or coal dust, both highly combustible, comes into contact with a heat source. Methane is a component of coal, and mining generates coal dust. The open flame of a carbide lamp can ignite either one and trigger an explosion. So can sparks from electrical equipment, or even just smoking a cigarette. The drier the air, the greater the risk, which is why mine explosions often happen on cold, dry winter days.

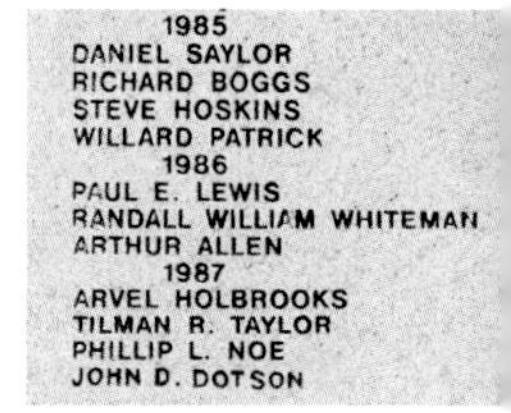

After an alarming number of explosions in British coal mines killed thousands of miners, inventors turned their attention to making safer lamps. In 1815, the eminent chemist Sir Humphry Davy designed one with a mesh screen that shielded the flame, keeping it contained. British coal companies adopted the Davy lamp, but it wasn't used in American mines, where explosions continued with some regularity.

There are various straightforward ways to deal with coal dust that, if taken together, help reduce the risk of explosions: Use exhaust fans to flush out the air, clean up the fine coal, wet down the area, and spread rock dust (typically pulverized limestone that absorbs thermal energy before it can trigger an explosion). At the Zero mine the last rock-dusting had been done about a year before, and the mine had never been watered down. The report that mine inspectors J.F. Davies and E.H. Hodgson released just six days after the explosion spelled out very clearly the many times the operators deviated from standard safety practices.

The Zero mine used an explosive called pellet powder. Ideally, the coal face is cut at the bottom. After that, the miner drills 6-foot holes into the

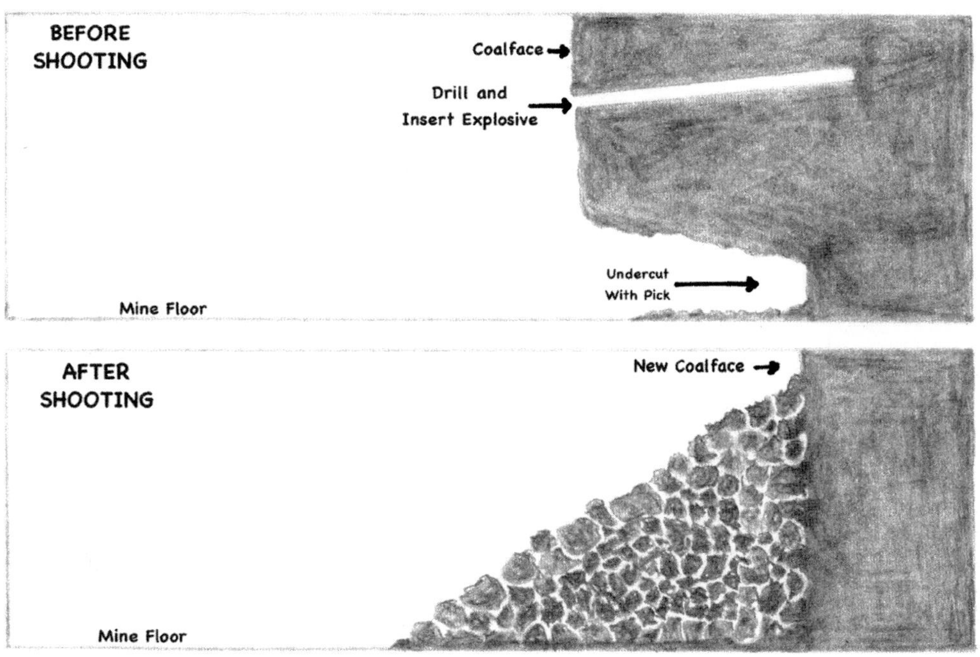

The coalface was undercut by the miner lying on his side, using a short pick.
Drawing by Laura Thomas

NONE 1988

face, inserts the powder pellets and then tamps the hole with clay. The force of the explosion takes the path of least resistance, and if all goes well, the coal just collapses onto the mine floor.

Failing to undercut the face before proceeding with the blast is called "shooting off the solid," and it increases the risk of a "windy shot," so called because rather than breaking the coal loose, the force of the explosion shoots back out through the drilled hole, expelling the tamping material as well as a blast of air into the mine—hence the name "windy." That's what happened on that fateful day at Zero.

The inspectors' report concluded that two shots had caused the explosion, the first one "probably having been a very windy shot throwing into suspension appreciable quantities of dust and occasioned most of the men to hasten to the entry from the working places." The second shot triggered the explosion.

And here's where things get iffy. The report continues, "Clay is presumably used for tamping. However, the two shots which caused the explosion had been tamped with dummies filled with fine coal dust, although the shots at the face of this room showed evidence of having been tamped with clay." The question is, how could the investigators possibly know what those openings were tamped with? All of the men mining in that area were killed, meaning there were no witnesses, and both shots would have kicked up large volumes of coal dust. So how could they know what had been used to tamp the charges?

Every other possible cause of the explosion can be traced to the careless and incompetent way the mine was run, but using fne coal to tamp a charge would be the sole responsibility of the now dead miner. If you read enough of these accident reports, you will see a pattern of blaming the victims.

After an accident, it is long-standing practice to get mines up and running again as soon as possible. So no one was surprised by the speed with which the investigation was concluded and a report released. Among its findings were:

- No pre-shift examination was made.
- The mine was filthy. "The active portion of the mine is very dry and dusty. The haulage roads showed evidence of considerable spilled coal, much of which was very fine."
- Evidence of coking showed that coal dust had caused the explosion. (Rapidly burning coal dust causes a layer of coke, i.e. partially burned coal, to coat the area where an explosion has taken place.)
- Explosives were found in several locations, including in an unsecured bin, indicating "gross ignorance or utter disregard of the hazards of careless handling and storage of explosives underground."
- A recommendation that "Shooting from the solid be positively prohibited."
- Open-flame "carbide lights are used by all persons underground."
- Ideally, experienced miners would fire all shots at night; instead, at the Zero mine, there was "shooting during the day when all men are in the mine, and evidently without proper supervision."

Despite all this, the authors concluded:

"The officials of the above-mentioned company are of the highest type and a group of persons who cooperate fully. This should be understood by all and this group of officials have been foremost advocates of safety for some time past, and this disaster was very disturbing to them, to say the least."

Nonetheless, the state mine inspectors insisted that there be some changes in the way the mines were operated, though this isn't mentioned in their report. One change was that explosives should be secured safely, rather than being randomly distributed throughout the mine. Another was that electric "Edison lamps" should be used instead of carbide lamps. Apparently, they could see that those six mines would always be covered with coal dust, so preventing open flames was a necessity.

According to an attorney who knew about the latter requirement, "Old man Guthrie was mad as hell. He knew he had to comply but he was determined not to pay for it." So Guthrie leaned on his old friend, the scrip system, to solve the problem.

The Harlan Fuel Co. had scrip pieces made that read "Light for One Shift Only." To get a battery-operated lamp, the miner had to authorize a deduction from his pay; in return, he'd get a token that would entitle him to use the lamp for that shift. Once the lamps were paid off, the company actually made money on the deal. They had transformed a safety requirement into a profit center!

To read the complete report, see Appendix B at harlanscrip.com.

The Three Point Explosion

A thousand yards away and 11 years later, that same coal seam exploded again. Mines may have different names, and be located in different coal camps, and yet tap the same seam of coal, which can run for miles. Harlan County has a number of coal seams, including the Harlan, High Splint, Low Splint, Kelloika, Wallins and McKnight. Both the Zero and Three Point mines worked the Harlan seam, and they had adjacent property lines.

Although the federal Bureau of Mines had previously labeled the Harlan seam "non-gassy"— and this despite having never conducted a gas inspection—the agency now said, "A gas explosion causing the death of 12 men occurred about 9 a.m. on Sept. 16, 1943, in the Three Point mine of the Three Point Coal Corp., Three Point, Kentucky." Six other miners were trapped for 14 hours before being rescued. The blast killed several men outright, burning and mangling their bodies. Others were suffocated by the gases produced by the explosion. There were 114 employees in the mine at the time of the accident.

The blast seriously damaged both the ventilation apparatus and the pumps, leading to flooding in the mine. The blast also broke down doors as much as 2,400 feet away, and tore loose a booster fan set in concrete and moved it 6 feet away. It derailed five empty cars. By the next day, workers had removed all the bodies.

Four days later, after the water had been pumped out, the inspectors launched an investigation to determine the cause. Throughout this period, the office of George S. Ward, secretary of the Harlan County Coal Operators Association, kept the press informed.

Bryson, mine superintendent J.C. Dawson, and two state inspectors searched the area. They found a burned matchstick that they claimed had survived not only the explosion but also the recovery of the bodies and the subsequent flooding. This, they maintained, was conclusive proof that the assistant foreman had caused the explosion by using that match to light a safety lamp. According to their official report:

"On Thursday morning, Sept. 23, Mr. Bryson telephoned the Norton office of the Bureau of Mines that he and the state inspectors had inspected the slant entry and recovered the disassembled nonpermissible safety lamp, the various parts of which were scattered over an area near the place where the assistant foreman's body was found. J.E. Bradburn and the writer left immediately for Harlan, Kentucky, and viewed the disassembled lamp in Mr. Bryson's office, where the various parts had been carefully kept separate as found. All parts of the lamp were thickly coated with a black smudge, due to their being submerged in water for several days, but the integral pieces were not in any other way damaged and could be readily assembled. This rather definitely proved that the lamp had been opened before the ignition, rather than blown apart by the explosion. A match box, containing several unburned wooden matches, and one match from which the sulphur had burned, found in the same area, were also exhibited. Mr. Bryson stated that the places where the various articles were found had been chalk-marked on the roof of the slant entry for the benefit of the Federal inspectors."

Thus, the determinative evidence concerning this accident was in the sole custody of an employee of the coal operators' association.

In the hurry to reopen the mine, the title of the final report of the inspectors misspelled Harlan County as "Harland County."

See Appendix C at harlanscrip.com for the U.S. Bureau of Mines report.

Charlie Thomas

CHAPTER 10

THE HARLAN COUNTY MINERS MEMORIAL

The Harlan County Miners Memorial, located on the grounds of the courthouse, lists the names of 1,340 men killed in accidents in the county's mines. Due to political considerations, those killed while attempting to unionize the workers aren't listed. And because of the difficulty of identifying them, black lung victims are not included either, although their numbers were significant.

Medical science has known about black lung disease since 1831, when a Scottish doctor named James Gregory first identified and described it. Nonetheless, it wasn't recognized by the operators, the states, or the federal government for many years. Tamping down the dust, ensuring proper ventilation, waiting until an area clears before resuming work, and wearing masks–all help prevent the disease, but these strategies cost money. The United Mine Workers of America fought for them, but because so many mines were not organized, a federal law was needed.

It took a tragedy to provoke change. In 1968, a mine in Marion County, West Virginia, blew up, killing 78 miners. The explosion was heard for miles, and flames shot 100 feet into the air. Nineteen bodies of the dead have never been recovered.

Mine No. 9, owned by the Consolidation Coal Co. (now Consol Energy), is located near the towns of Farmington and Mannington, leading some to refer to the explosion as the Farmington Disaster and others as the Mannington Disaster.

Bonnie E. Stewart wrote a book about it called *No. 9: The 1968 Farmington Mining Disaster*. Her extensive analysis of this and other mine tragedies caused her to conclude:

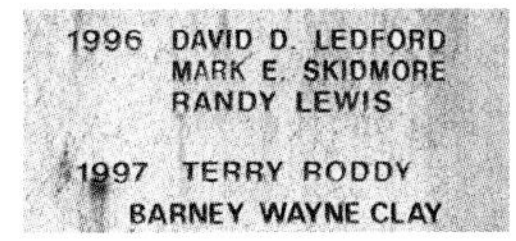

> I can say with confidence that rarely, if ever, are coal mine disasters accidents. Historically, at least during the past century, most mine disasters have been the result of poor management, inadequate regulation and enforcement, greed, negligence, carelessness, foolishness, selfishness, complacency, indifference—add your own descriptor. All too often, the drive to produce coal—to make money, to meet contracts, to satisfy stockholders—has trumped safety.[84]

More succinctly, Hazel Dickens wrote a song about it:

> *Remember the disaster at the Mannington mine,*
> *Where seventy-eight miners were buried alive,*
> *Because of unsafe conditions, your daddy died.*

The rescue attempts continued for a week, and TV reporters from all the major networks kept the viewing public aware of the story. As a result of all this publicity, Congress passed the 1969 Coal Mine Safety and Health Act. Years of work by the United Mine Workers and black lung victims had finally paid off; one part of the law mandated compensation for miners diagnosed with black lung, and for their families when the miners died.

Explosions get the big headlines because they often involve multiple casualties, but most accidental deaths in the mines stem from "roof falls," commonly called "slate falls." Occurring in ones and twos and threes, they mount up over time to make coal mining historically the most dangerous job in the country. Since the federal government started keeping count in 1900, about 105,000 miners have died in U.S. mines.[85]

A roughly equal number, however, have died of pneumoconiosis, or black lung disease. If it were possible to identify those fatalities, the Harlan County memorial would have to be twice as big. And for every actual death in the mines, there are more than 15 disabling injuries.[86] So in addition to those names on the memorial, another 20,000 or so Harlan County miners most likely sustained serious injuries. The impact on the miners' families is significant—one more factor in the high poverty rate in Harlan and the coal fields generally.

The memorial was conceived in 1985 as a project of the local chapter of the Junior Chamber of Commerce. The organization's members are typically business professionals, but at that time the chapter's president, Randy

Head, was a coal miner. And when Jaycees Jerry Laws and Rick Boggs died in a mining accident that year, the chapter decided to build a memorial not just to them but to all whose lives had been similarly cut short. 1998 JEFFREY RAY BOWMAN GARY MERRILL

After obtaining permission from the county's fiscal court to erect the memorial on the courthouse grounds, the club held a competition to determine what it would look like. David Harp's graceful design—a broken cross with engraved black granite plaques—easily won out.

Courtesy of State University of New York Press, from *Two Sides to Everything* by Shaunna L. Scott. Used by permission.

Perhaps inspired by the Vietnam Veterans Memorial, at ground level the monument would appear to be disjointed walls of names, but from the upper stories of the courthouse, the cross shape would be revealed.

1999
NONE

The dedication ceremony was set for Memorial Day—May 31, 1986—largely because, traditionally, that has been when Harlan County natives return to decorate graves and visit friends and relatives. The engravers had promised to meet that deadline, but two days before, word came that the name plaques would not be ready. The club decided to go ahead with the ceremony with only the framework for the plaques in place.

The featured speaker was U.S. Senator Wendell Ford, who had played no part in either planning or funding the memorial. A few other politicians also gave speeches, as did a representative of the Kentucky Department of Mines and Minerals.[87] Without exception, they spoke glowingly about the safer working conditions that they said had now been established in the mines—the result, they maintained, of teamwork on the part of miners, mine owners and the state.

Strikingly absent from this "team," however, was the United Mine Workers union, which many miners and industry analysts alike credited with being the driving force in improving U.S. mine safety.[88]

"David Zegeer from the federal Mine Safety and Health Administration continued in the vein. Pointing to a recent downward trend in mine fatalities, he credited the many parties who were instrumental in securing safer working conditions for miners. It seemed that everyone *but* the United Mine Workers had stormed the barricades to demand protection of the miners' health and safety."[89]

UMW representatives were neither invited nor mentioned. According to sociologist Shaunna L. Scott, who was involved in the planning for the memorial, Jaycee members said it would be "too risky" to include union officials in the ceremony, because the "word around town" had been that certain Jaycees would find themselves unemployed if even a single United Mine Workers official "set foot on the speakers' platform."[90]

> "After the ceremony ended, miners and their relatives went back to their family holiday festivities. Visiting dignitaries were escorted to the local country club, where the Harlan County Coal Operators Association provided them with refreshments."[91]

Sometime after the ceremony, the plaques arrived and were installed. The club members had researched county records and newspaper files to compile a list of the names of the dead, but either through their errors or those of the engravers, several names had been misspelled.

As a result, the Harlan County Fiscal Court (the local equivalent of county commissioners) had the memorial rebuilt. Rather than use the original design, however, they erected a single monument with names engraved on each side. That is the one that is there today, and names have continued to be added as needed. The plaques from the first memorial are stored at the Portal 31 miners' museum in Lynch.

I.D. PLATES: These brass plates, displaying the worker's name and Social Security number, helped identify miners' bodies after an accident. Like soldiers' dog tags, they came in pairs, both worn on the belt. In the event of a fatality, one was removed by the recovery team and the other left on the body. Brass is non-sparking, an important safety consideration in a coal mine. From the author's collection

In 1972 the US Navy honored the county by naming a Newport class ship the *U.S.S. Harlan County*. She was a tank landing ship with a capacity of 29 M-48 tanks. She was decommissioned in 1995. US Navy

AFTERWORD

An archaeology student who was passing through a small island chain decided, on a whim, to spend the night on one of them. It was small, roughly rectangular in shape, and there were many similar islands nearby. There was green everywhere, one hill after another, with meandering streams below and high peaks above. Paradise.

The inhabitants were widely said to be hostile, suspicious and violent. But though they spoke a distinctive dialect, he encountered only friendliness, and so began to chat with those he met. One old man showed him some worn metal artifacts containing various inscriptions. The man had eight or 10 of the tokens and offered them for sale. Although the student didn't know what they were, each was slightly different, and he bought them as souvenirs of his visit.

As far as he knew, these pieces were unknown in the wider world, so he stayed on in hopes of finding more. Every time he thought he'd assembled a complete collection, someone came up with yet another piece of stamped metal—maybe copper this time, or nickel, rather than brass, and with slightly different markings. Before long he had gathered 120 different examples and identified about 30 specific points of origin for them, so he decided it was time to return to school and see if his professors could shed any light on what he'd found.

Back in the city, the student was surprised to learn that a small group of amateur archaeologists was, in fact, well aware of the artifacts and had managed to learn quite a bit about them. Together, they had identified not 120 but over 900 different kinds from Island One, as the student had come to think of it. Similar pieces had been produced on perhaps 100 other

2005
RUSSELL COLE, SR.
BRANDON LEE WILDER
DAVID MORRIS, JR.
2006
RICK McKNIGHT
AMON BROCK
JIMMY B. LEE
ROY MIDDLETON
GEORGE WILLIAM PETRA
PARIS THOMAS, JR.

islands, amounting to several thousand distinct types in all. Still, they were mostly ignored by those scholars whose specialty was studying this particular island culture. The few books about the tokens had been written by the collectors and privately published, and some were out of print.

I am that curious student, and Harlan, where I grew up, is Island One. This book would not have been possible without the tireless efforts of the archaeologists collectively known as the National Scrip Collectors Association. In 1971, one of their number, Gordon Dodrill, self-published a book called *20,000 Coal Company Stores*, and the club itself publishes catalogues listing all the scrip they've found. These researchers have lovingly saved and catalogued the artifacts for decades, and have helped me immeasurably in my attempts to understand exactly what that old man held in his hand and what it meant.

For the most part, archaeologists study civilizations by examining the surviving artifacts. What are they? How were they used? What is their significance? For the study of prehistorical times, those primary sources are the only kind of evidence there is. For the mine wars, though, there is an abundance of secondary sources. In the case of Harlan, we can turn to the many books that have been written about events there, as well as extensive newspaper coverage. Yet we should not lose sight of that primary source: Coal scrip. More study is needed into the scrip system and its impact on the mountain counties.

When news reporters journeyed to the coal fields in response to an explosion, a strike or a deployment of the National Guard, that triggering event was typically their sole focus. But if, instead, they had chosen to come in peacetime and stay awhile, they might have dug deeper and perhaps expanded the scope of their reporting to include things like scrip—and that, in turn, might have spurred professional historians to research the origins of those tokens, and ponder their meaning. As things stand, however, the best book on Harlan's history, which I have quoted extensively in these pages, is John W. Hevener's *Which Side Are You On?: The Harlan County Coal Miners, 1931-39*, and it mentions scrip only once, referencing a 1931 National Miners Union demand for "payment of wages in cash rather than scrip."[92]

EMPTIES: Empty coal cars during the county-wide, 1939 strike at Wisconsin Steel's mine at Benham, Kentucky. University of Kentucky

In the 1939 strike, the National Guard engaged in mass arrests, in this case hauling the strikers in a cattle truck. University of Kentucky

2018
HUBERT "BUBBY" GRUBBS, JR

When major corporations like Ford, U.S. Steel, Peabody, Koppers, and Chicago Edison decided to make eastern Kentucky their next big business opportunity, they came equipped with a model that had been tested for decades. It called for constructing towns entirely owned by the company, strict policing by armed mine guards, gaining the cooperation of the local sheriff, a near absence of civil rights, establishing a company store—and scrip.

The overriding idea was that mining was, and would remain, a low-wage endeavor. Every industry tries to rein in labor costs, but the coal operators' goal seems to have been to eliminate payroll altogether, reducing their workforce to a level of dependence and impoverishment that we don't expect to see in modern society.

There were many ways to reduce miners' pay, the most obvious one being a wage cut. But a more insidious tactic involved levying a steady stream of seemingly "reasonable" charges: for sharpening a pick, having a doctor on call, and covering such essentials as house rent, coal for heating and carbide for lamps. Still other schemes included refusing to pay miners for necessary cleanup work, shorting the weight on the scales, and maintaining a long pay period that forced families to get advances in scrip just so they could survive until the next payday. The coal operators did not invent wage theft, but they were very good at it, and the impact is still felt many years later.

The union opposed all of these company strategies, and so the companies worked hard to keep the union out. They consistently made organizing as difficult as possible. The guards, the fences, the company-owned towns; all interfered with a union man's ability to communicate with miners in other camps. And with the local sheriff in their pocket, the operators were free to break up union meetings, send in spies, fire union workers, and even bomb churches where union meetings were held. They beat up, arrested and killed innocent people who were exercising their right to organize.

A truly independent local government would not allow the most flagrant of these operator tactics, so it's not surprising that many coal counties saw their court systems, as well as their sheriff's departments, taken over by the companies. And the operators' quest to co-opt county government did not rely solely on the usual "lying to get elected" ploy that voters everywhere have come to expect. More blatant crimes such as vote buying, ballot stealing and trading favors for official acts were all common.

The National Guard was called in repeatedly to halt election fraud. In 1935, 1,400 National Guard members were dispatched to Harlan to police the gubernatorial primary, and they returned that fall to police the general election.[93] Note that these guardsmen were called not to police a strike, but solely to prevent fraud at the ballot box when a governorship was at stake. When the same fraud occurred in pursuit of local offices, nobody stepped in.

The 1939 Strike[94]

On April 3, 1939, a nationwide coal strike began, shutting down almost every mine in the country. Every Harlan mine closed, and the daily shipments from the county plummeted from 1,500 rail cars per day to zero. By May 13, most of the country's operators had signed union contracts. The seven Southern associations held out for a week, but then all of them signed—except Harlan.

The lone industrywide holdout, the Harlan County Coal Operators Association refused to sign contracts. But when the Whitfields tried to reopen their mine at Kitts, hundreds of pickets converged and prevented it. Mine after mine would open for one day, only to be closed by massive picketing the next day.

Finally, on May 15, the governor sent in the National Guard. The soldiers blocked pickets who were coming in from Virginia and Tennessee, dispersed picketing miners, and arrested miners by the hundreds. The First Amendment guarantees the right to peaceably assemble, yet the Guard charged the miners with "banding and confederating." And though the soldiers shot and killed two miners and wounded several others, the miners refrained from retaliating.

The United Mine Workers supported the strikers, and finally, after a 15-week strike, most of the Harlan mines signed the contract.

ASSOCIATED PRESS PHOTO BERLINER BUERO

Waffenfunde bei Streikenden !

ASSOCIATED PRESS BILD zeigt Offiziere der Nationalgarde
bei der Untersuchung der zahlreichen bei Streikenden gefundenen
Waffen in Harlan im Staate Kentucky, USA, am 13. Juli 1939.
Die Träger dieser Waffen wurden verhaftet, im ganzen beträgt
die Zahl der Inhaftierten inHarlan 250 .
NAP 52466 26.7.39 TWO EX SCKGHFIAENN

Associated Press Photo Berlin Bureau

Weapons found among strikers: Associated Press photo shows officers of the National Guard in Harlan, Kentucky while investigating the numerous weapons found on strikers in Harlan, Kentucky, on July 13, 1939. Those carrying these weapons were arrested. In total, the number of those imprisoned in Harlan is 250.

News of the coal wars spread internationally. While the point of the Guard's display of seized weapons was to say that the pickets were well armed, in fact that is not very many weapons for hundreds of pickets to have. Note too that possession of these guns was not illegal.

THE SCRIP GALLERY

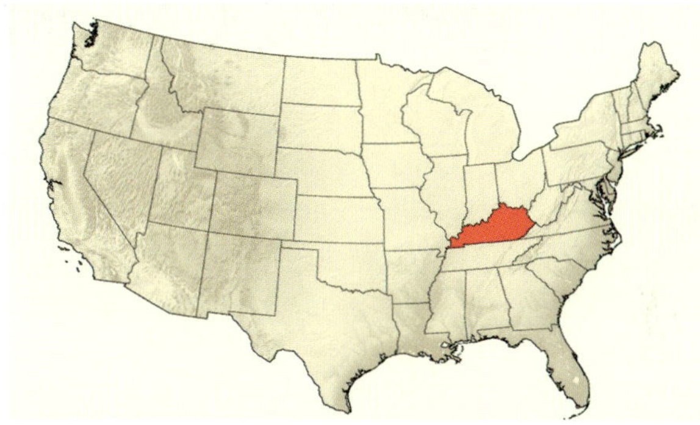

Kentucky

Harlan County

Mine closures had begun after World War II as demand lessened and as the more readily accessible coal in the Western states, particularly Wyoming, started coming online. And when the mines closed, so did the company stores, meaning scrip no longer served a purpose.

The remaining stocks of scrip were sometimes sold for scrap, tossed into a river or buried in the mine that was being decommissioned. Other times, the company essentially abandoned its scrip, which then wound up in the hands of anyone who happened to be in the area. Those pieces are generally still easy to find.

Harlan County occupies a small corner of a smallish state, making it even more remarkable that so much scrip was used there.

At least 110 coal companies in Harlan used scrip. Together, they issued at least 976 different pieces of scrip. Pictured in this book are 798 different metal pieces and 16 different paper pieces.

There were 135 known tokens for which we could not obtain photographs. As we obtain photos of those pieces we will list them on the website harlanscrip.com. Any corrections will be noted on the site as well.

A complete, and probably unattainable, collection of Harlan County scrip would total about 976 pieces.

Tokens are listed first by town or coal camp, and then by company. The numbers assigned to the coal camps, and the different series of the scrip pieces, are the numbers used by the National Scrip Collectors Association (www.scripcollectors.org). The club has twice-yearly meetings where members buy, sell and trade scrip. Scrip can sometimes be found at antique shops, coin shops or flea markets. Nowadays, most scrip is sold on eBay or other on-line auction houses.

Here are some prices for Harlan scrip sold on eBay in the fall of 2023:

- 10¢, Crummies Creek Coal Co., Crummies, KY, $2.95
- 5¢, Harlan Collieries, Brookside, KY, $5.50
- 1¢, Black Star Coal Co., Alva, KY, $6.50
- 10¢, Clover Fork Coal Mining Co., Kitts, KY, $9.95
- 1¢, Harcrow Mine, Evarts, KY $10.00
- 5¢ & 10¢, Yocum Creek Coal Co., Evarts, KY $12.95
- 50¢, Harlan Coal & Coke, Ridgeway, KY, $17.16
- 5¢, Bardo Coal Mining Co., Bardo, KY, $17.49
- 1¢, Kentucky King Coal Co., Lisle, KY, $42.66
- 1¢, Bardo Coal Mining Co., Bardo, KY, $81.00
- $1.00, Harlan Coal & Coke, Ridgeway, KY $102.50
- 10¢, Cornett-Lewis Coal Co., Lisbon, KY, $355.00
- 50¢, Harlan Liberty Coal Co., Evarts, KY, $510.00
- 25¢, Dixie Darby Coal Co., LeJunior, KY, $588.00
- 10¢, Evarts Coal Co., Evarts, KY, $1,025.00

A collection of the most common pieces from Harlan (or any other coal mining county) can be started for a modest sum. Rare pieces sell for substantial sums, which is ironic because while researching this book, I repeatedly came across stories about miners who literally never saw any actual currency at all. By the time payday came around, their entire earnings had been converted into scrip just to feed their families. Johnny Cash sang a song about it:

Ain't never got acquainted with a dollar bill,
And I don't ever reckon that I ever will.
A dollar ain't made for a feller, I'm told,
That scoops up a livin' loadin' coal.
Loadin' coal, loadin' coal, loadin' coal...[95]

Overgrown chimneys at the Chevrolet coal camp. Ken Allen

The L&N Don't Stop Here Anymore.[96] Ken Allen

Coal Camps

Index of Companies

Ages 29

Named for Ages Creek, itself named for a local family.

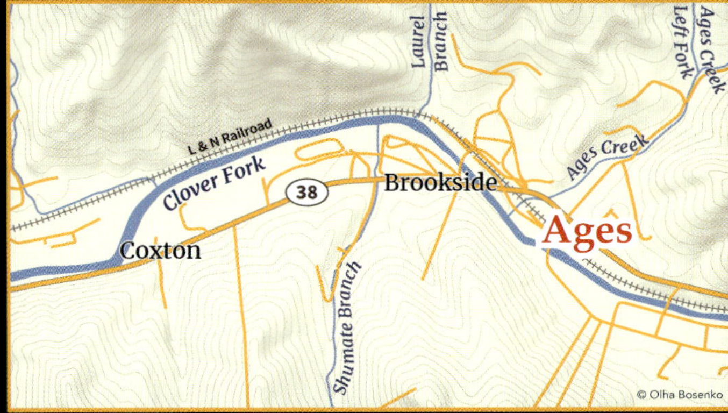

Ages Supply Co.

Not shown: B5, B25

B50

Howard Fortune

East Harlan Coal Co.

Not shown: C100

D10

Tommy Skeens

D100

Tommy Skeens

E5

Ken Allen

C10

Howard Fortune

A25

Howard Fortune

A50

Howard Fortune

A100

Ken Allen

Alva 75

When the 1931 strike started, 60 miners went on strike at Black Star Coal and they and their families were evicted from their homes. When miners held meetings in the community church, it was burned down.

Black Star Coal Co.

Not shown: A10b, E100a, E100c, B1c,

Burley Williams

A5a
Ken Allen

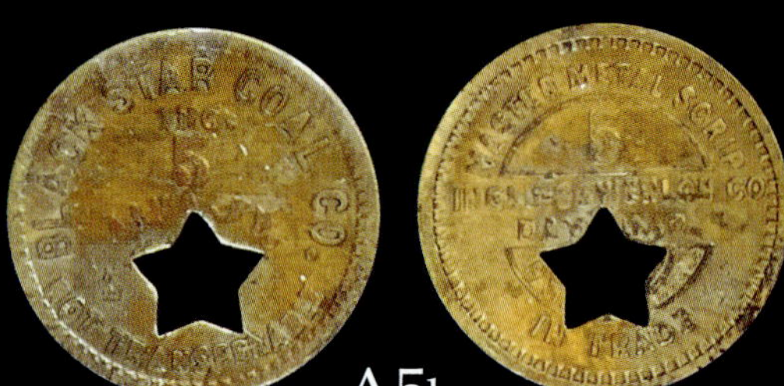
A5b
Steve Calwell

A10a
Frank Sutton

A25
Frank Sutton

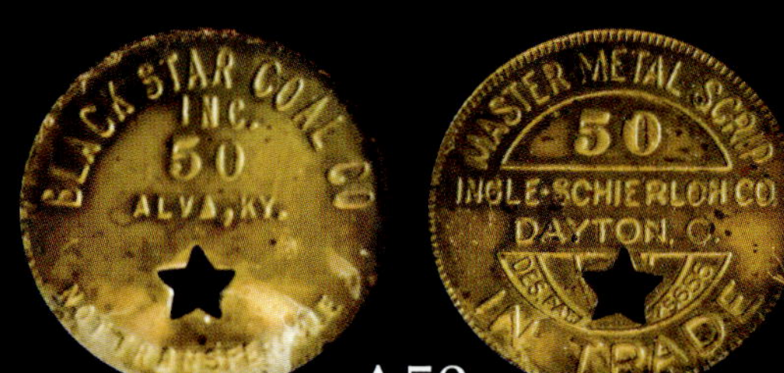

A50
Frank Sutton

A100
Frank Sutton

E100b
David Schenkman

B1a
Ken Allen

B1b
Ken Allen

B5
Ken Allen

B10
Ken Allen

B25
Frank Sutton

B50
Frank Sutton

B100

C1
Ron Saylor

D1

F5

Banner Fork
151

Fordson Coal Company

Not shown: A1, A25, A100, B1c, B1d, C5, I1

Fordson Coal Co. was owned by the Ford Motor Co.

A5
Ken Allen

A10
Howard Fortune

A50

B1a
Ken Allen

B1b
Ken Allen

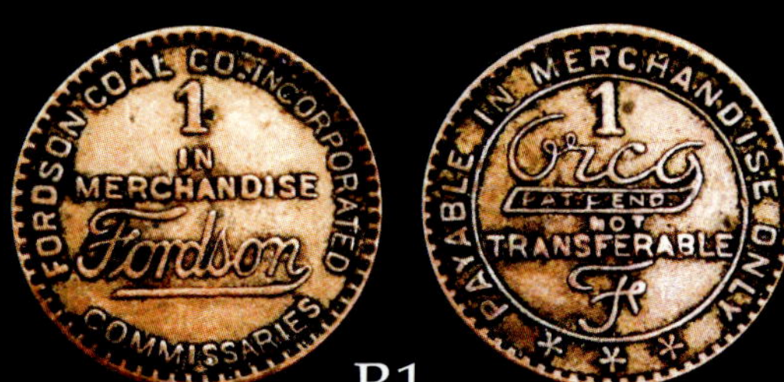

B1e
Louisville Numismatics Exchange

B5a
Ken Allen

B5b

B5c

Ken Allen

B10a

Ken Allen

B10b

B25

Ken Allen

B50

Billy Campbell

B100

Ken Allen

B500

D100

Billy Campbell

E1

Ken Allen

F1

Ken Allen

Bardo 155

Named after Bordeaux, France, by coal operator James Bowling who had served in France during WWI.

Bardo Coal Mining Co.

During the 1931 strike, the National Guard placed a machine gun nest on top of the Bardo Coal Mining Co. commissary.

C1

C5

C10

C25

Frank Sutton

C50

Bowling Coal Mining Co.

A5
Frank Sutton

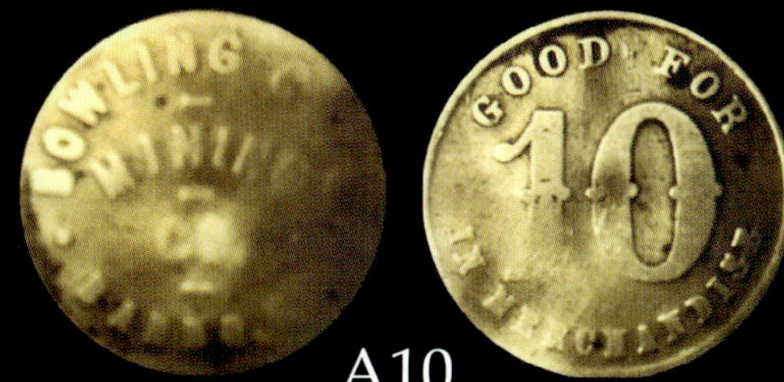

A10
Frank Sutton

A25
Frank Sutton

A50
Frank Sutton

A100
Frank Sutton

B5
Frank Sutton

B10
Frank Sutton

B25
Frank Sutton

B50
Frank Sutton

B100
Frank Sutton

Benito 219

Benito Supply Co. (Company store for Benito Harlan Corp.)

A5

A10

A25
Ken Allen

A100
Ken Allen

A50

Ken Allen

Black Joe 287

Harlan-Fox

A5

A10

Frank Sutton

Bland 301

R.C. Tway Coal Co.

Not shown: D100

R. C. Tway was an officer in the HCCOA, and was indicted for conspiring to deprive miners of their constitutional rights. Tway signed Sheriff Theodore Middleton's bonds and had the Commonwealth Attorney on a $2100 annual retainer, giving him leverage over those public officials.

A5

A10

A25

A50

B100

Howard Fortune

C100

David Mullins

Brookside

385

Named for being between two brooks.

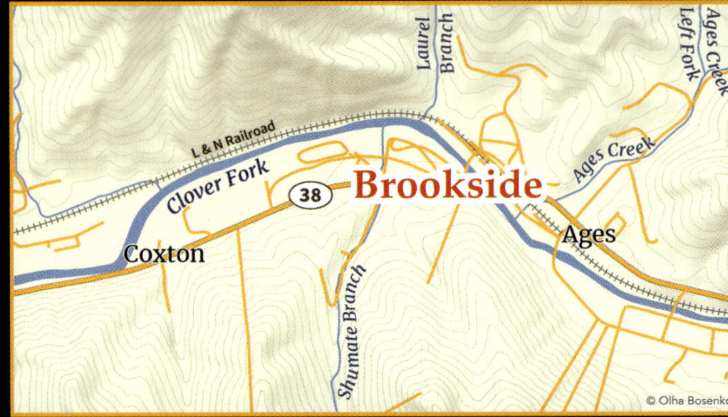

Harlan Collieries Co.

Not shown: A100b, B25a

Harlan Collieries employed 300 men and was owned by Bryan Whitfield who also owned the Harlan Country Club where National Guard troops camped during the 1931 strike.

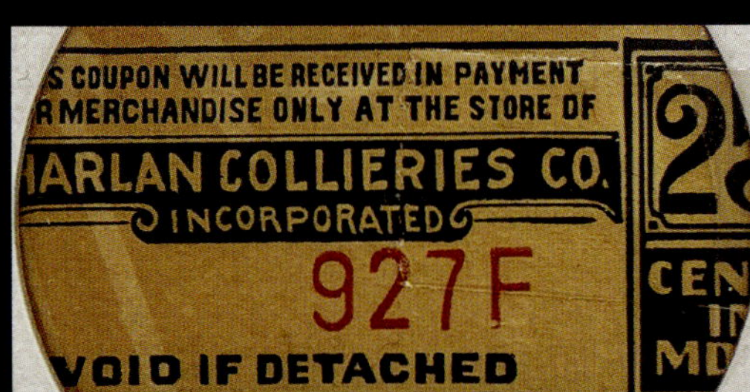

Paper scrip from the Burley Williams Collection

A5a

Frank Sutton

A5b

A10a
Steve Cawood

A10b
Steve Cawood

A10c
Ken Allen

A25a
Frank Sutton

A25b
Ken Allen

A50

A100a
Frank Sutton

A100c
Steve Cawood

B5a
Ken Allen

B5b
Ken Allen

C5
Steve Hayden

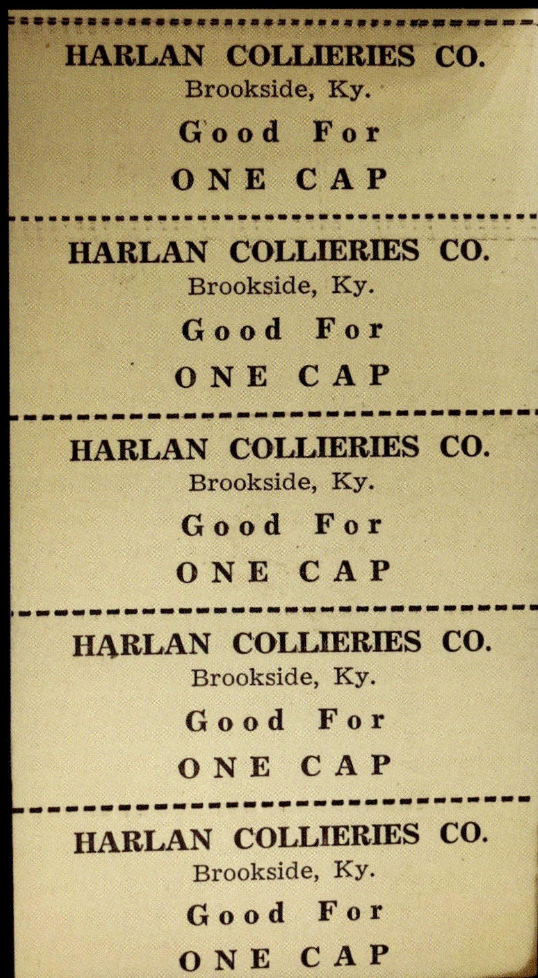

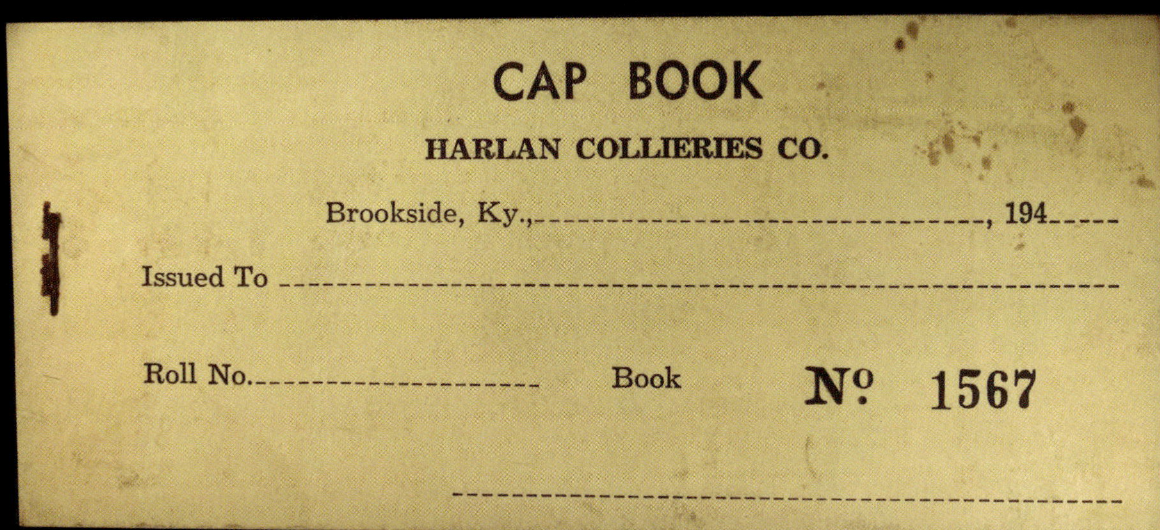

Blasting cap book courtesy of Burley Williams

Cawood 511

Named for the Cawood family whose progenitor was Berry Cawood (1758-1848), a Revolutionary War hero.

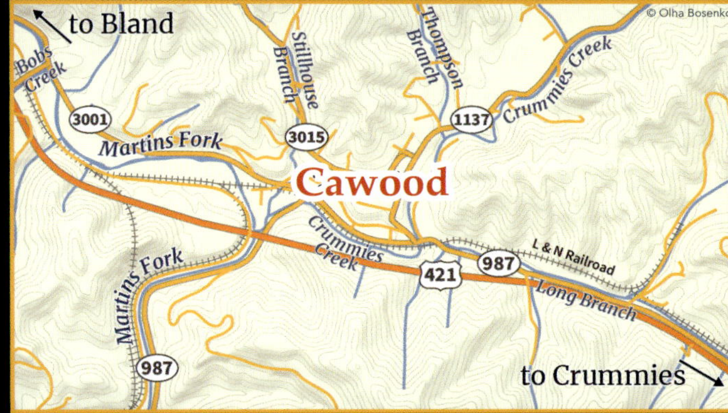

Crummies Creek Coal Co.

In 1941, mine guards/deputies at Crummies Creek Coal Co. killed 4 union members who had stopped by the commissary for refreshments.

A10

Frank Sutton

A5

A25

A50

A100

Ellis Knob Coal Co.

Not shown: B5b, B50

B5a
Steve Cawood

B10a
Steve Cawood

B10b
Steve Cawood

B100a
Steve Cawood

B100b
Ken Allen

Brett Kennard

B100b

Ken Allen

A25

Chevrolet
541

The brother of the owner of the Blue Diamond Mine wrecked his 1917 Chevrolet nearby and left it abandoned there.

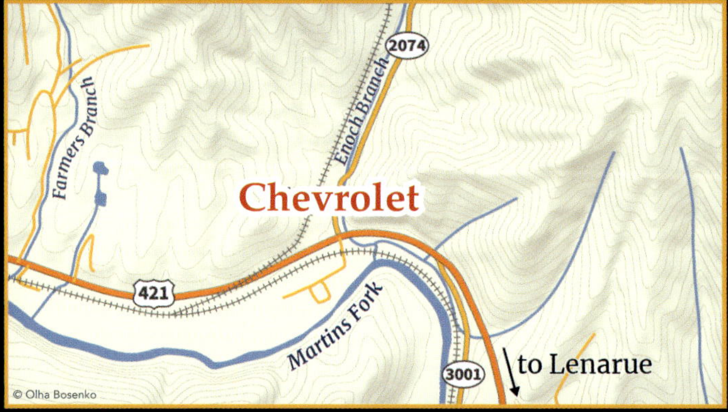

Blue Diamond Coal Co.

Not shown: C5b

D10
David Mullins

C5a

C10a
Burley Williams

C10b
Ken Allen

C100a
Steve Cawood

C100b
Burley Williams

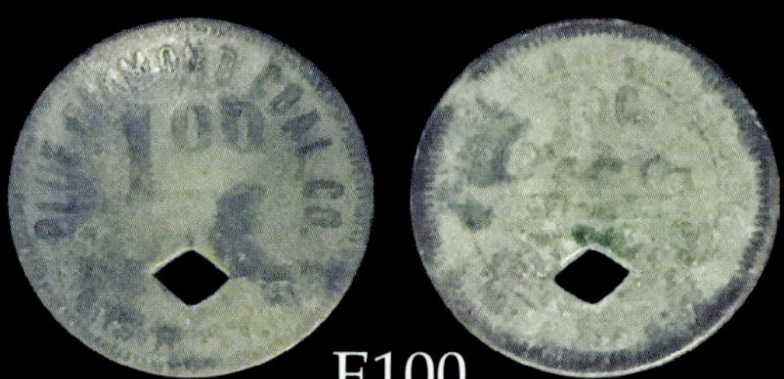

E100
Burley Williams

Crown Coal Co.

A5
Frank Sutton

A10
Frank Sutton

A25a

A25b

A50

A100

Harlan Superior Coal

Not shown: B5

Closplint
587

Named after the Clover Splint Coal Co.

Clover Splint Coal Co.

Not shown: A100b

In 1933 the church where miner and minister B.H. Moses held union meetings was destroyed by dynamite.

A5a
David Schenkman

A1
Howard Fortune

A5b
Howard Fortune

A10a
Howard Fortune

A10b
Howard Fortune

A25
Howard Fortune

A50
Howard Fortune

A100a
Howard Fortune

A500
Howard Fortune

Coalgood

609

Mary Helen Coal Co.

Not shown: H5, H10, G25, G50, G100b, A50a, A100d

F5

Steve Cawood

F10a

Howard Fortune

F10b

Howard Fortune

F10c

Nick Fugate, Shawn Fugate

F100

Howard Fortune

G100a

A5b
Ken Allen

A5a
Brett Kennard

A10

A25a

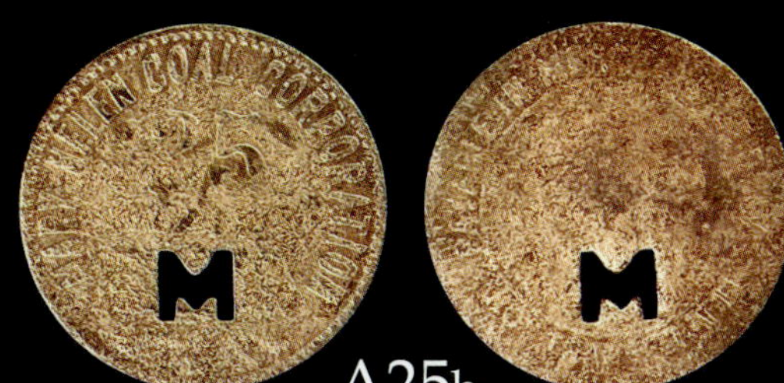

A25b
Steve Cawood

A25c
Steve Cawood

A50a
David Mullins

Mary Helen Coal Co. continued

A50b

Ken Allen

A100a

A100b

Steve Cawood

A100c

Steve Cawood

A2000

B5

Frank Sutton

C100

Pure D. Coal Company

Not Shown: E5b, E5c

E5a
Ken Allen

E10

E25
Ken Allen

E50
Ken Allen

E100

PAYABLE IN MERCHANDISE ONLY
50
OTCO
REG. U.S. PAT. OFF.
THE OSBORNE REGISTER CO.
CIN. O. U.S.A.
NOT TRANSFERABLE

A50b

MARY HELEN COAL CORP.
50
COALGOOD, KY.

Cote 673

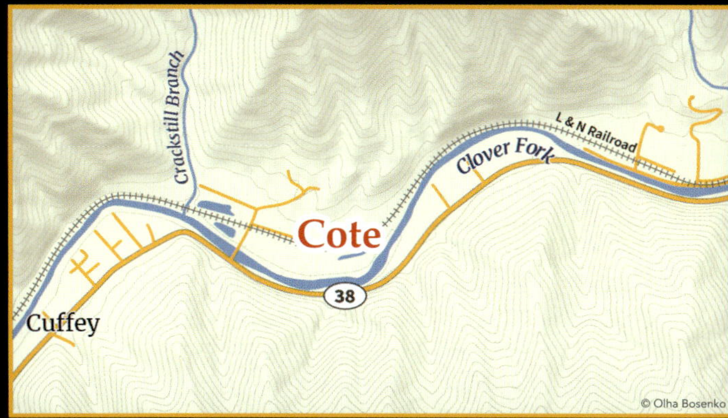

River Ridge Collieries

A5
Frank Sutton

A10

A25
John Slusher

A50

A100

B1
Frank Sutton

Coxton 681

Chestnut Ridge Supply Co.

Not shown: B50, B100, C50b

Company store for Melcroft Coal Company

B1

Steve Cawood

B5

Steve Cawood

B10a

Ken Allen

B10b

Ken Allen

B25

Steve Cawood

Koppers Stores

Not shown: G10b

C5
Billy Campbell

C10
Ron Saylor

C25
Ken Allen

C50a
Ken Allen

D5a
David Mullins

D100
David Mullins

D5b
Ken Allen

Koppers Stores continued

E1a
David Mullins

E1b
Burley Williams

E1c
Burley Williams

E5a

E10

E25

E50
Frank Sutton

E100

E500

F1

F5
Billy Campbell

F10
Steve Cawood

F25
David Mullins

G1
Ken Allen

G5
Ken Allen

G10a
Ken Allen

G25
Ken Allen

G50
Ken Allen

G100
Ken Allen

Koppers Stores continued

H1
Ken Allen

J1
Ken Allen

K1
Ron Saylor

L1
Ken Allen

M1a
Howard Fortune

M1b
Billy Campbell

N1
Billy Campbell

O1
Steve Cawood

P1
Ken Allen

I1c
Ken Allen

I1a
Ken Allen

I1b
Howard Fortune

I1d
David Mullins

I1e
Steve Cawood

Koppers Stores continued

Burley Williams

CAR CHECK
Frank Sutton

Lick Branch Coal Co.

A5
Frank Sutton

A100
Frank Sutton

Crummies

705

Named by early settlers after a herd of bison whose horns were crumpled rather than straight.

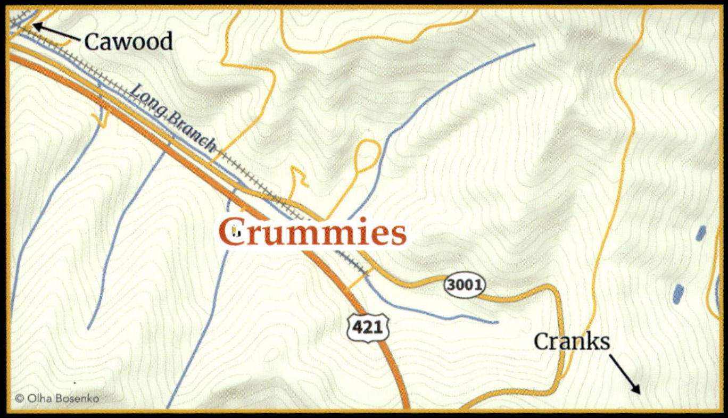

Crummies Creek Coal Co.

Not shown: B50c

A5
Frank Sutton

A10
Frank Sutton

A25
Frank Sutton

A50
Frank Sutton

A100
Frank Sutton

Crummies Creek Coal Co. continued

B5

B10a

Ken Allen

B10b

B25a

Ken Allen

B25b

B50a

Steve Cawood

B50b

B100a

Ken Allen

Crummies Creek continued

B100b

E50

Ken Allen

C1a

C1b

Ken Allen

C1c

D1

Ken Allen

Cuffey 711

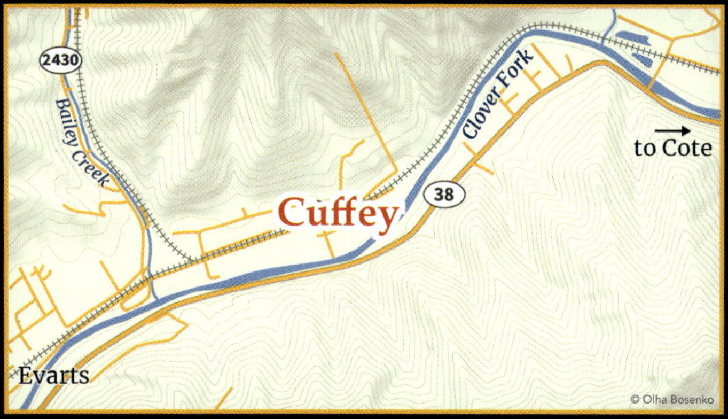

Standard Harlan Coal Co.

not shown: A10, A100

A50

Draper 839

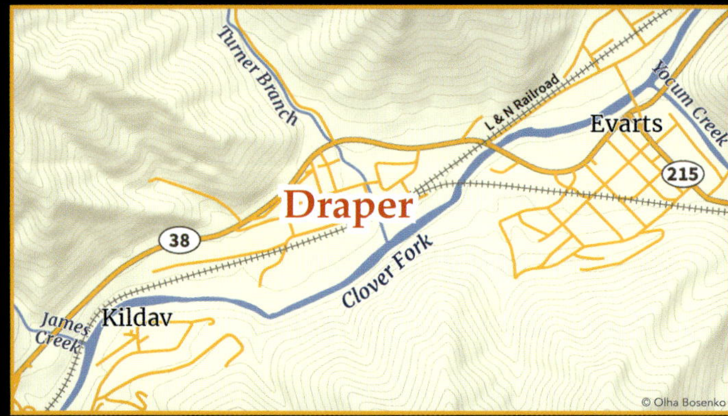

Draper Mercantile Co. (Company Store for J.L. Smith Coal Co.)

B5

B10

Steve Cawood

B50

Howard Fortune

B100

East Harlan Coal Co.

A10

Ken Allen

A5

A25

A50

A100

Elcomb 889

The McComb Coal Co.

Not shown: A10

A5
Howard Fortune

A25

A50
Steve Cawood

A100
Steve Cawood

Evarts 975

Evarts was the site of the Battle of Evarts where three deputies and one pro-union miner were killed.

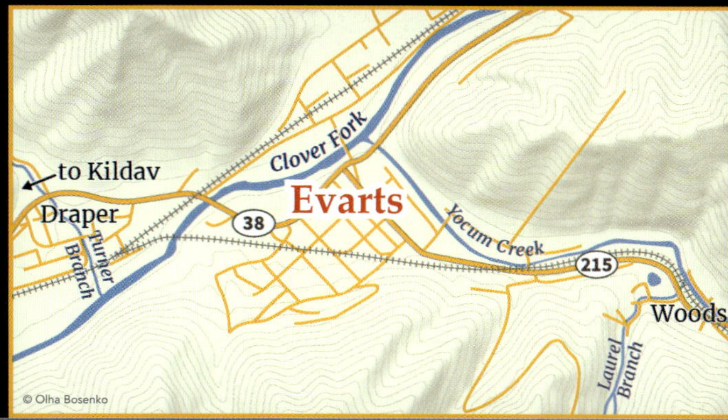

Black Mountain Coal Corporation

Not shown: M100b

M100a
Tommy Skeens

Darby Coal Co.

A5
Steve Cawood

Evarts Coal Co.

Not shown: K100

K10
David Mullins

Harcrow Mines

I5

I10

I25

I50

I100

Harlan Co-Operative Coal Co.

Not shown: C25

C5

Steve Cawood

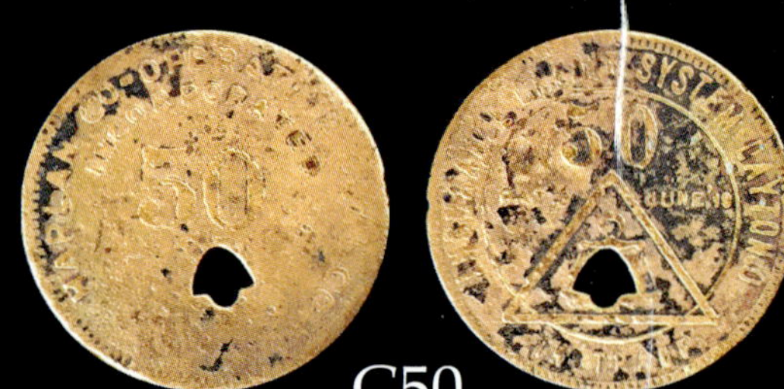

C50

C100

Steve Cawood

Harlan-Kellioka Coal Co.

D5
Ken Allen

D10
Howard Fortune

D25
Howard Fortune

D100

Harlan Liberty Coal Co.

Not shown: L1, L50, L100, B50, B100

B5

Howard Fortune

B25

Steve Cawood

B10

Frank Sutton

Rye Hollow Coal Co.

N5

Howard Fortune

Springton Coal Co.

F5
Howard Fortune

F10
Steve Cawood

F25
Frank Sutton

F100
Howard Fortune

F50
Ken Allen

Sugar Camp Mining Co.

Not shown: G5, G10b

G10a
Steve Cawood

G25

G50a
Frank Sutton

G50b
Steve Cawood

G100
Ken Allen

Superior Harlan Coal Co.

Not shown: E25

E1

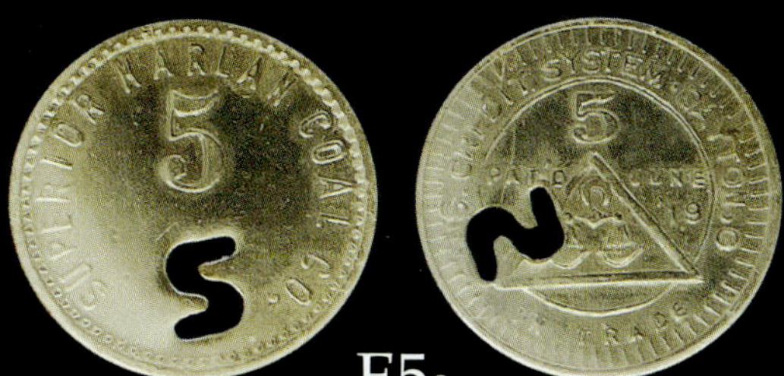

E5a
Howard Fortune

E5b
Steve Cawood

E10
Howard Fortune

E50
Steve Cawood

E100
Steve Cawood

Turner Fuel Co.

J5

J10

J25

J50

J100

Yokum Creek Coal Co.

H5a

H5b

H25

H50

Hester Butterfield

Gaston 1101

Named after Harlan Gas Coal Co.

Harlan Gas Coal Co.

Not shown: A25

A10
Ken Allen

A50
Ken Allen

Harlan Town Coal Co.

Not shown: B10

A50

Ken Allen

Grays Knob
1169

Named for a nearby elevation, itself named after early settlers.

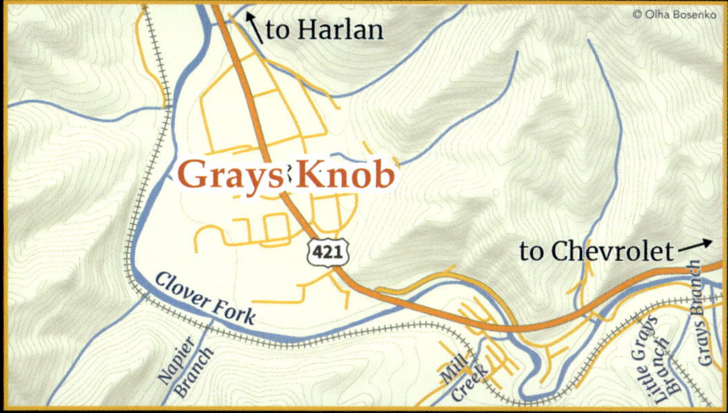

Wilson-Berger Coal Co.

Not shown: C100b

A5

Frank Sutton

A10

A25a

Ken Allen

A25b

Frank Sutton

A50

A100a

Wilson-Berger Coal Co. continued

B5
Steve Cawood

B10
Steve Cawood

B25
Ken Allen

C5
Ken Allen

C10

C25
Frank Sutton

C50
Ken Allen

C100a

Harlan 1231

Named for Major Silas Harlan who was killed at the Battle of Blue Licks during the Revolutionary War. Sometimes known locally as Harlan Town. Earlier called Spurlock, then Mt. Pleasant, then Harlan Courthouse, and finally in 1865, Harlan.

Catrons Creek Coal Co.

Catrons Creek was shown as Katherines Creek on early maps.

E5
Tommy Skeens

E10
Tommy Skeens

E25a
Ken Allen

E25b
Tommy Skeens

E50
Tommy Skeens

E100
Tommy Skeens

Clover Fork Coal Co.

K5
Frank Sutton

K10
Frank Sutton

K25
David Mullins

K50
Frank Sutton

Elcomb Coal Co.

I1
Frank Sutton

I5
Frank Sutton

I10

I25

I50

I100

J100

Ken Allen

Harlan Home Coal Co.

F25

Howard Fortune

F50

Howard Fortune

F100

Howard & Ingram

Not shown:, G25, G100

G5
Steve Cawood

G10
Howard Fortune

G50
Howard Fortune

S.C. Saylor

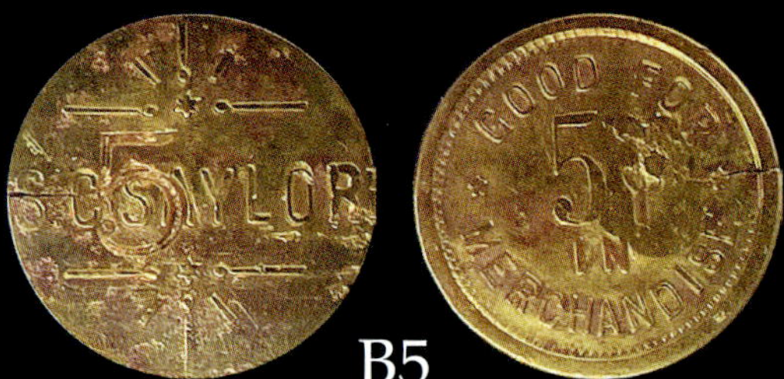

B5
Steve Cawood

B10
Steve Cawood

B25
Steve Cawood

B50
Steve Cawood

B100
David Mullins

Shawnee Gas Coal Co.

not shown: A50, A100, L25a, L25b, L100

A5
Ken Allen

A10
David Mullins

A25
Howard Fortune

L5
Steve Cawood

L10
Steve Cawood

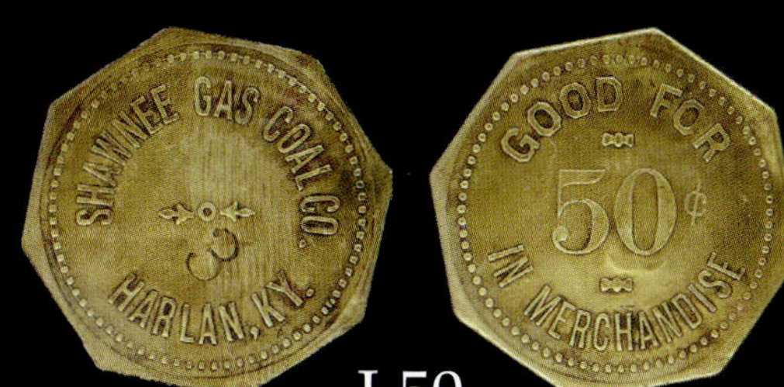

L50
Howard Fortune

Wallins Creek Comet Mine Collieries Co.

Not shown: M5, N50, N100

M25
Steve Cawood

M100
Ken Allen

High Splint
1323

Formerly called Seagrave.
Named for the High Splint Coal Co.

High Splint Coal Co.

Not shown: A5b, A10c, B100a, C5c

A5a
Ken Allen

A10a
Ken Allen

A10b
Ken Allen

A25a
Steve Cawood

A25b
Steve Cawood

A25c
Louisville Numismatic Exchange

A50
Steve Cawood

A100
Ken Allen

B1
Frank Sutton

B10a
Brett Kennard

B10b
Ken Allen

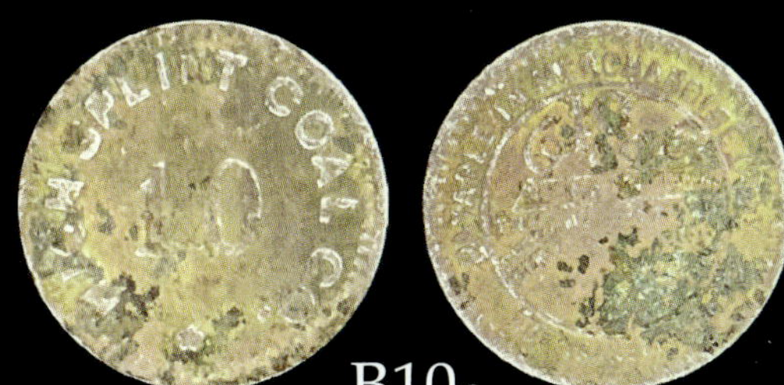

B10c
Steve Cawood

B25

B50a

B50b
Steve Cawood

B100b

High Splint Coal Co. continued

C1
Ken Allen

C5a
Ken Allen

C5b
Steve Cawood

D500

Seagraves Coal Co.

E5

E10

E25

E50

E100

Insull 1405

Formerly known as Fee. Named for Samuel Insull, the president of Chicago Edison, which owned the Southern Mining Co.

Southern Mining Co.

Not shown: A25c, D1b

A5a

A5b
Ken Allen

A10

A25a

A25b
Ken Allen

A50

A100a
Ken Allen

A100b

B1
Ken Allen

B10
Ken Allen

C5a
Van Cortlandt

C5b

C10
Ken Allen

F1
Ken Allen

D1a

E1

Kellioka
1487

Named for John Kelly, a mine owner.

Kellioka Coal Co.

Not shown: A25, A100, B5

A5

David Mullins

A10

Ken Allen

A50

Howard Fortune

B5

Ken Allen

B10
Ken Allen

B25
Ken Allen

B100
Ken Allen

B50
Ken Allen

Kentenia
1497

Named for parts of the names of Kentucky, Tennessee, and Virginia.

Banner Fork Coal Co.

A5
Ken Allen

Kentucky King Coal Co.

Not shown: B5

B25
Ken Allen

Kenvir 1499

Named for Kentucky and Virginia by the Peabody Coal Corp. The road alongside Yocum Creek goes only as far as Punkin Center and does not pass into Virginia. Local people would not have named a new town "Kenvir," but to someone in an office in Chicago, it must have seemed fitting.

The Black Mountain Corporation

Not shown: B50, E25

Black Mountain's deputized mine guards killed a number of union members, and at least four of these guards were killed themselves.

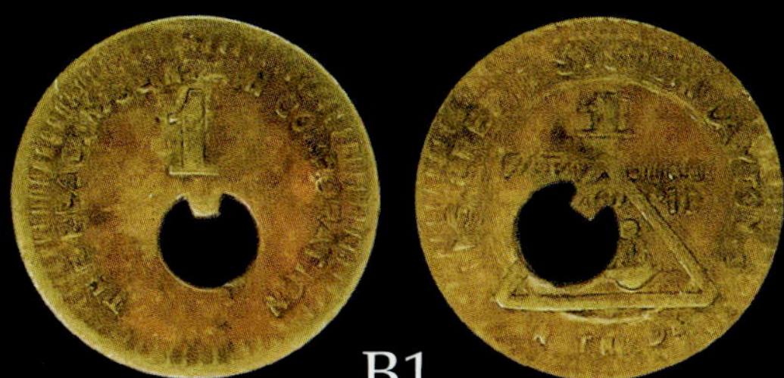

B1

Howard Fortune

B5

William Jones

B10

Steve Cawood

B25

Tommy Skeens

B100

Ken Allen

The Black Mountain Corporation continued

C5a
Steve Cawood

C5b
Ken Allen

C10

C25
Tommy Skeens

C100
Ken Allen

D5a
Ken Allen

D5b
David Mullins

D5c
Ken Allen

D10
Ken Allen

The Black Mountain Corporation continued

A10
Ken Allen

A1

A25

A50

A100
David Mullins

A100

This copy of A100 was made by Peabody in 1983 to commemorate the 100th anniversary of their founding.

A5

Kildav 1511

Named for Killebrew and Davis, owners of the King Harlan Co.

King-Harlan Co.

Not shown: B100, D100

A5

A10

A25

A50

A100

Frank Sutton

B5a
Steve Cawood

B5b
Ken Allen

B5c
Ken Allen

B5d
Steve Cawood

B5e
Ken Allen

B10a
Ken Allen

B10b

B10c
David Mullins

King-Harlan Co. continued

B25b
Tommy Skeens

B25a
Ken Allen

B50
Ken Allen

C5
Ken Allen

GOOD FOR
50¢
IN MERCHANDISE

A50

KING-HARLAN CO. INC.
KILDAV.
KY.
WRIGHT CIN'TI. O.

Kitts 1535

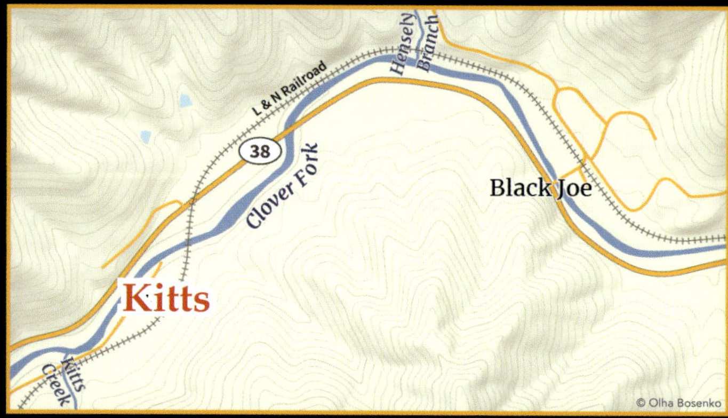

Clover Fork Coal Co.

Not shown: B10b

B5
Ken Allen

B1

B10a
John Slusher

B25

B50
Steve Cawood

C100a
Ken Allen

C100b

Golden Ash Coal Co.

A5
Ken Allen

A10
Frank Sutton

A25
Frank Sutton

A50
Frank Sutton

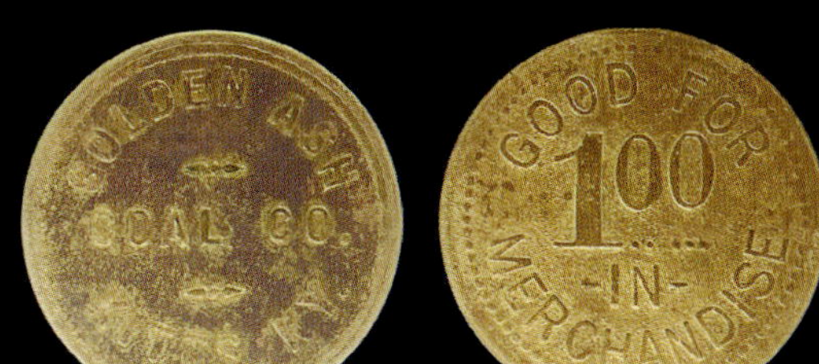

A100
Howard Fortune

D5

Tommy Skeens

D10

Tommy Skeens

D25

Tommy Skeens

D50

Tommy Skeens

D100

Tommy Skeens

Tommy Skeens

LE JUNIOR

E50b

Ken Allen

Le Junior
1605

Named by postmaster and mine owner Leander Bowling, Sr. for his infant son, Leander, Junior.

Benito Mining Co.

Not shown: E25

E1
David Mullins

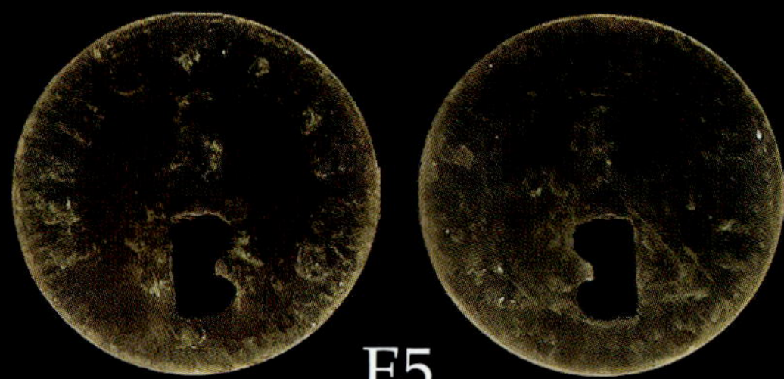

E5
Howard Fortune

E10
Steve Cawood

E50a
Tim Howard

E50b
Ken Allen

E100a
Steve Cawood

E100b
Frank Sutton

Berger Coal Mining Co.

not shown: A10a

A5
Howard Fortune

A10b
Howard Fortune

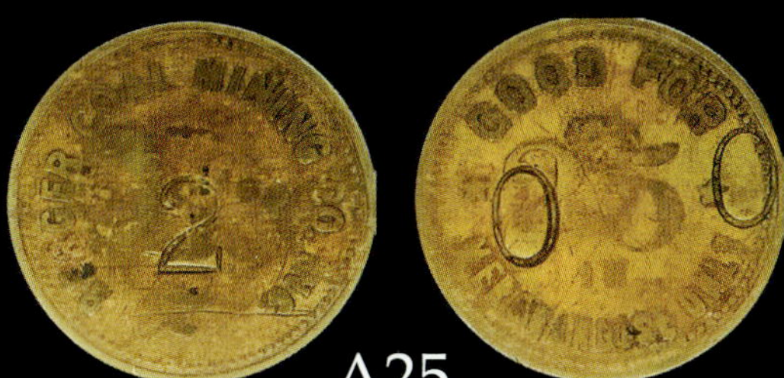

A25
Howard Fortune

A100a
David Mullins

A100b
Ken Allen

Berger Coal Mining Co. continued

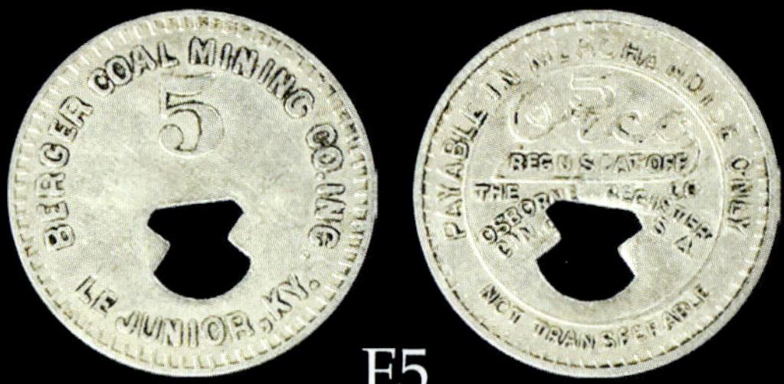

F5

F10

F25

F50

F100

G5a
Frank Sutton

G5b
Ken Allen

G10
Frank Sutton

G25
Frank Sutton

G50
Frank Sutton

G100

Bowling Mining Co.

not shown: L50

B50
Randy Salyers

B100
Howard Fortune

Cook & Sharpe Coal Co.

not shown: H5b

D5

Frank Sutton

D10

D25

D50

D100

H5a

H10

H25

H50a

Steve Cawood

H50b

Steve Cawood

H100

I1

Dixie Darby Coal Co.

K25
Steve Cawood

K50
Steve Cawood

K100
Ken Allen

Home Supply Co. (Company store for P.V. & K. Coal Co.)

not shown: J5c

C5
Ken Allen

C10
Ken Allen

C100
Ken Allen

J1

J5a
Howard Fortune

J5b
David Mullins

J10

J25b
Ken Allen

J25a
Ken Allen

J50
Steve Cawood

J100
Frank Sutton

Lena Rue
1607

Also called Rue or Glidden.

Mine owner Frank F. Cawood named this camp for his daughter, Lena Rue.

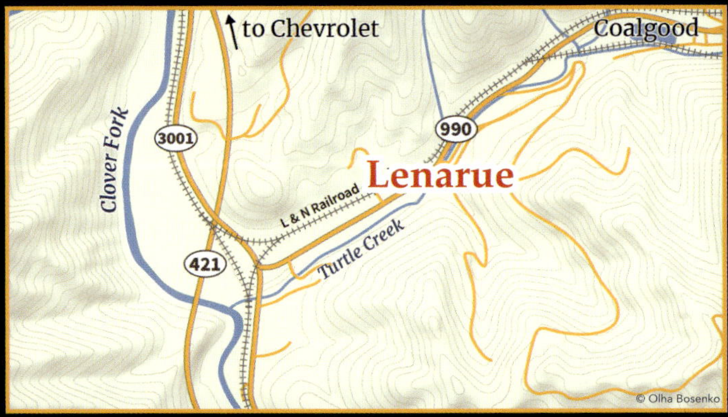

Lena Rue Coal Co.

Not shown: B10

A5
Steve Cawood

A10
Steve Cawood

Lick Branch
1627

Three Point Coal Co.

Not shown: B50

A5

A10

Liggett 1635

Perkins-Harlan mine owner Floran D. Perkins named this coal camp after his wife's family name.

Perkins-Harlan Coal Co.

Not shown: B5, B10a, B10b, B25a

B25b

Ken Allen

C25

Ken Allen

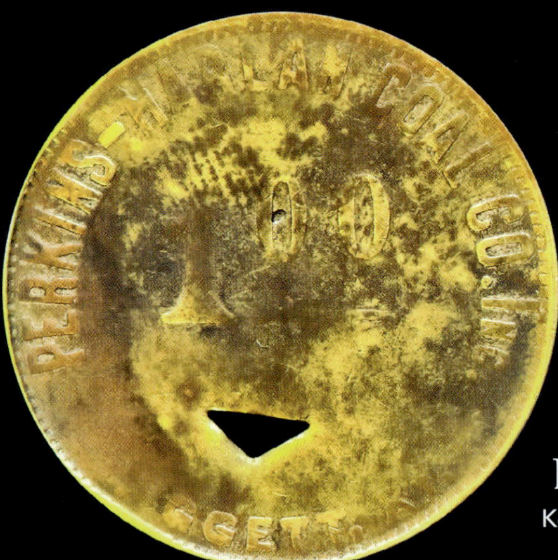

B100

Ken Allen

A1a

A1b

A5a

A5b
Ron Saylor

A10
Ron Saylor

A25

A50

A100

Lisbon 1648

Now called Louellen.

Also known as Closplint No. 2.

Cornett-Lewis Coal Co.

A5

Steve Cawood

A10

Ken Allen

A25

Ken Allen

Lisle 1649

Kentucky King Coal Co.

Not shown: A10a, A10b, A25a, A25b, A50, A100

A5a
Ken Allen

A5b
Steve Cawood

A10c
Ken Allen

A25c
Tommy Skeens

B1

Burley Williams

Louellen

1683

Formerly called Lisbon. Named by the president of Cornett-Lewis Coal Co., Denver B. Cornett, for his daughter, Lou Ellen.

Cornett-Lewis Coal Co.

Not shown: B50, B100a, B500, I50

A5
Frank Sutton

A10
Ken Allen

A25
Frank Sutton

A50
Steve Cawood

G5
Ken Allen

G10
Steve Cawood

G50
Howard Fortune

F100
Ken Allen

B100b
Ken Allen

C5
Ken Allen

C10
Frank Sutton

C50
Steve Cawood

H100a
Steve Cawood

H100b
Steve Cawood

Cornett-Lewis Coal Co. continued

D1

Ken Allen

E5

Ken Allen

E10

E25

E50

E100

E500

Lowe 1689

© Olha Bosenko
Left Fork
Turtle Creek
Turtle Creek
990
Coalgood
Right Fork Turtle Cre
Lowe
Cranks Creek Lake

Lynch 1728

Named for U. S. Steel president
Thomas Lynch

U. S. Steel Corporation

(U.S. Coal & Coke Corporation was U.S. Steel's subsidiary at Lynch. Their company store was called The United Supply Company.)

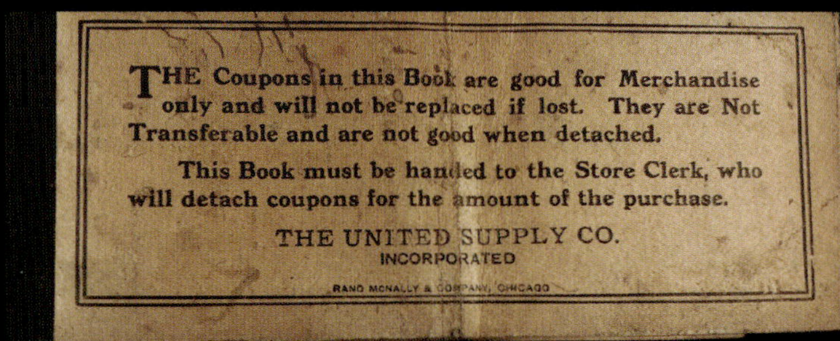

THE Coupons in this Book are good for Merchandise only and will not be replaced if lost. They are Not Transferable and are not good when detached.

This Book must be handed to the Store Clerk, who will detach coupons for the amount of the purchase.

THE UNITED SUPPLY CO.
INCORPORATED

RAND MCNALLY & COMPANY, CHICAGO

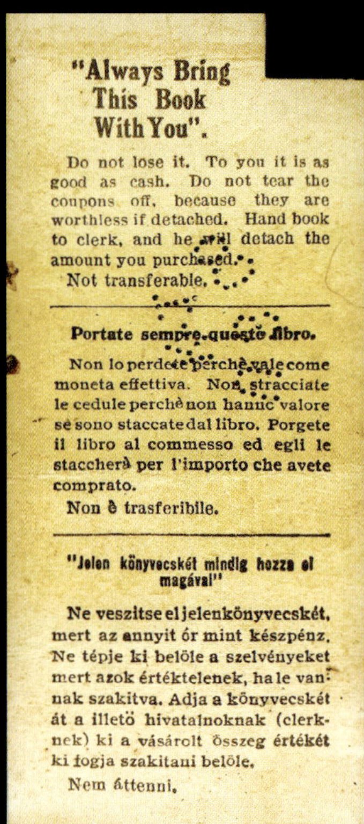

"Always Bring This Book With You".

Do not lose it. To you it is as good as cash. Do not tear the coupons off, because they are worthless if detached. Hand book to clerk, and he will detach the amount you purchased.
Not transferable.

Portate sempre questo libro.

Non lo perdete perchè vale come moneta effettiva. Non stracciate le cedule perchè non hanno valore se sono staccate dal libro. Porgete il libro al commesso ed egli le staccherà per l'importo che avete comprato.
Non è trasferibile.

"Jelen könyvecskét mindig hozza el magával"

Ne veszitse el jelenkönyvecskét, mert az annyit ór mint készpénz. Ne tépje ki belöle a szelvényeket mert azok értéktelenek, ha le vannak szakitva. Adja a könyvecskét át a illetö hivatalnoknak (clerknek) ki a vásárolt összeg értékét ki fogja szakitani belöle.
Nem áttenni.

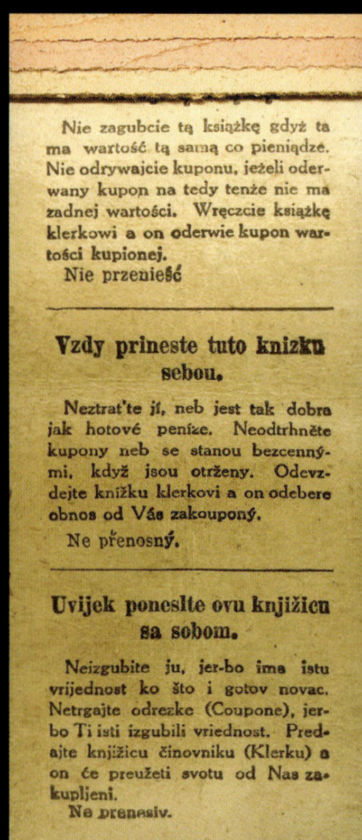

Nie zagubcie tą książkę gdyż ta ma wartość tą samą co pieniądze. Nie odrywajcie kuponu, jeżeli oderwany kupon na tedy tenże nie ma żadnej wartości. Wręczcie książkę klerkowi a on oderwie kupon wartości kupionej.
Nie przenieść

Vzdy prineste tuto knizku sebou.

Neztrat'te jí, neb jest tak dobra jak hotové peníze. Neodtrhněte kupony neb se stanou bezcenný-mi, když jsou otrženy. Odevzdejte knížku klerkovi a on odebere obnos od Vás zakoupený.
Ne přenosný.

Uvijek ponesite ovu knjižicu sa sobom.

Neizgubite ju, jer-bo ima istu vrijednost ko što i gotov novac. Netrgajte odrezke (Coupone), jer-bo Ti isti izgubili vriednost. Predajte knjižicu činovniku (Klerku) a on će preuzeti svotu od Nas zakupljeni.
Ne prenesiv.

U.S. Steel put the instructions for using the scrip coupons in six languages: English, Italian, Hungarian, Polish, Czech and Slovenian.

U.S. Steel paper scrip courtesy of Ron Saylor

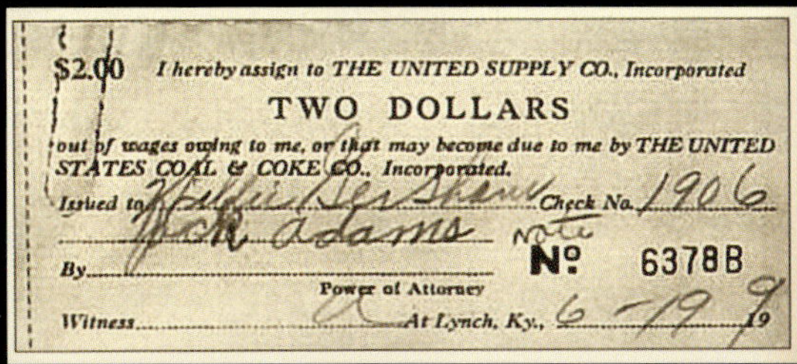

Courtesy of portal31.org

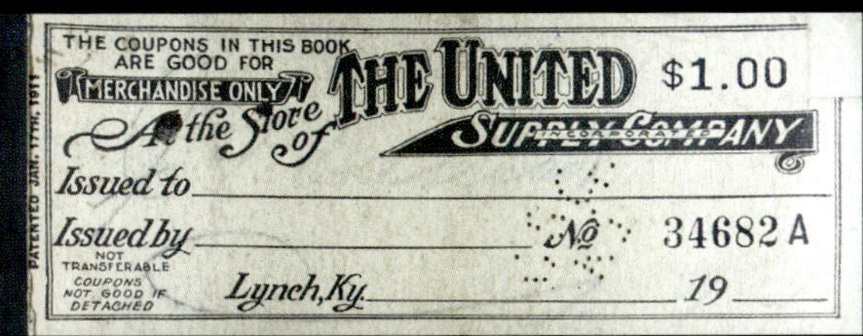

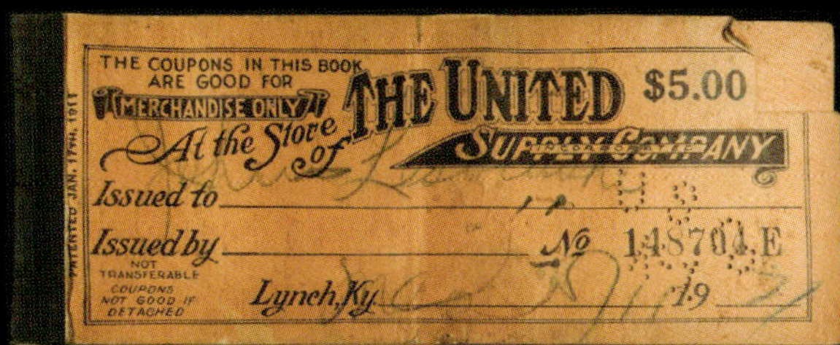

Paper scrip courtesy of Ron Saylor

U. S. Steel Corporation continued

Burley Williams

Brett Kennard

Brett Kennard

Malcolmson

1755

Named for Alexander Y. Malcomson, owner of Malcomson Coal Co. and one of Henry Ford's business partners.

Green Silvers Coal Co.

During his tenure as sheriff, Theodore Middleton became the owner of Green Silvers Coal, owned stock in Crummies Creek Coal, and a one fourth interest in Verda Supply Co.

E1

Harlan Gas Coal Co.

Not shown: F5

A5

Steve Cawood

B5

Harlan Gas Coal Co. continued

C5
Ken Allen

C10

C50

C100
Ken Allen

D10a
Ken Allen

D10b
Steve Cawood

C25
Ken Allen

Mary Alice
1805

Named by H. K. Buttermore, owner of Mary Alice Coal Co. for his daughters, Mary Jane and Ruth Alice.

Mary Alice Supply Co.
(Company store for Mary Alice Coal Co.)

Not shown: A100c

A5

A10a

A10b

A25a

A25b
Ken Allen

A50

A100a

A100b
Steve Cawood

Molus 1939

It was in the Molus coal camp that Florence Reece wrote "Which Side Are You On?" in 1931. Her husband, Sam Reece, worked in the mines there and was active in organizing for the National Miners Union.

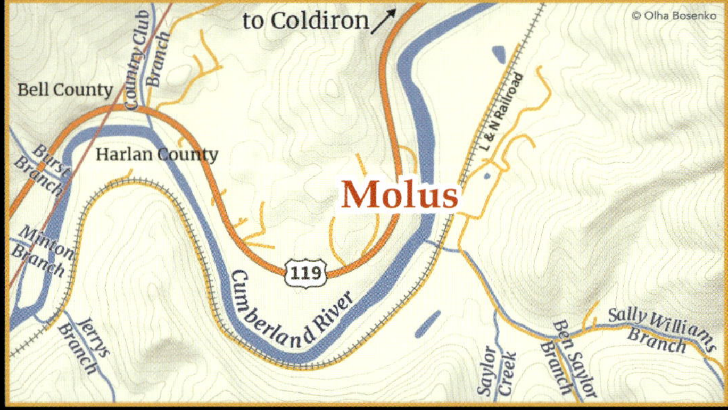

Molus Coal Co.

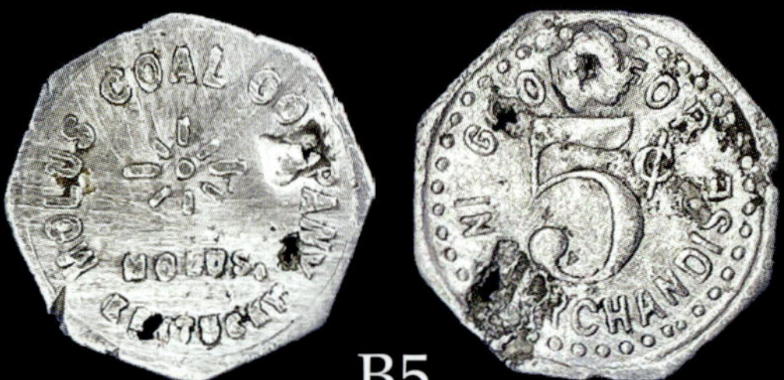

B5
Steve Cawood

B10
Ken Allen

Molus Supply Co. (Company Store for Molus Coal Company)

A5
Ken Allen

A10
Ken Allen

A50

A100

A25
Ken Allen

Sanborn Supply Co.

Not shown: E10, E25b

E5
Howard Fortune

E25a
Ron Saylor

E50
Ken Allen

Morris Saylor

Not shown: C25

After Morris Saylor was elected County Judge, he was enriched by acquiring a one third interest in coal land leased to Harlan-Wallins Coal Corp. and a quarter interest in Verda Supply Co.

C5
Steve Cawood

C10
Ken Allen

C50
Ken Allen

John P. Saylor General Md'se

Not shown: D25, D100

Company store for Harlan Wallins Coal Corp.

D5
Ken Allen

D10
Ken Allen

D50
Ken Allen

B10

Ken Allen

Nolansburg
2081

Later named Splint.

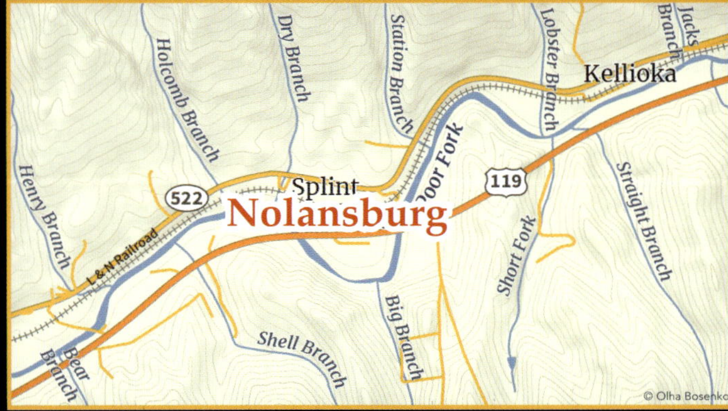

Harlan Splint Coal Company

not shown: A10, A50

A1
Howard Fortune

A5
Steve Cawood

A25
Ken Allen

The Kellioka Coal Co.

B10
Ken Allen

B25
Ken Allen

B100
Howard Fortune

Path Fork
2185

Blue Diamond Coal Co.

A1
Ken Allen

A5a
John Slusher

A5b
Burley Williams

A10
Frank Sutton

A25

A50

Blue Diamond Coal Co. continued

A100

Frank Sutton

Willis Harlan Coal Co.

Not shownL B10, B25, B100

B5

Howard Fortune

LUMBER SCRIP

Brett Kennard

Pee Vee 2197

Named for Postmaster Perry V. Cole.

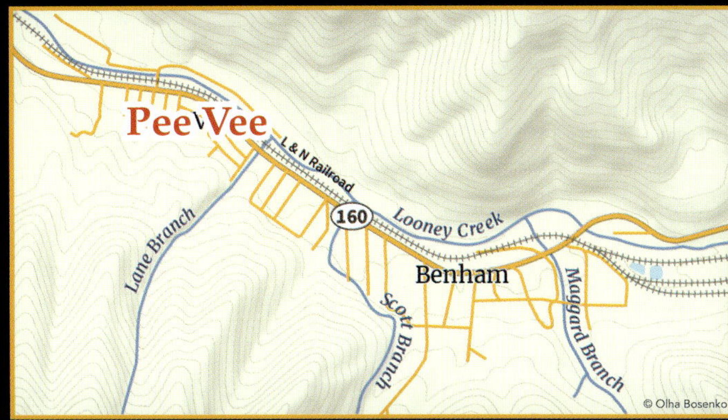

C.E. Flanary Store

Not shown: C5

B5

B10

B25

B50

B100

Loony Creek Coal Co.

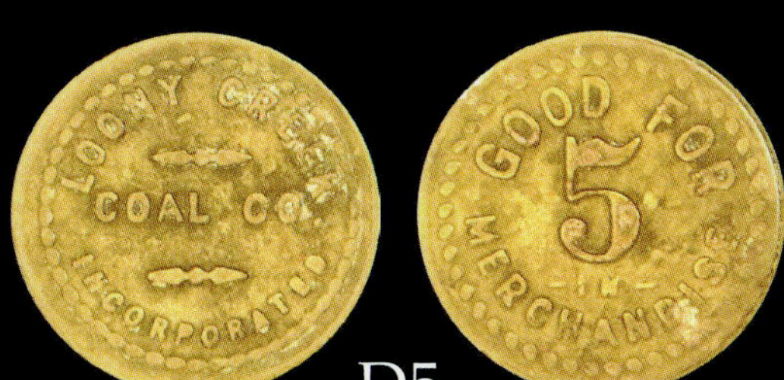

D5

Ken Allen

A5

Ken Allen

Putney 2317

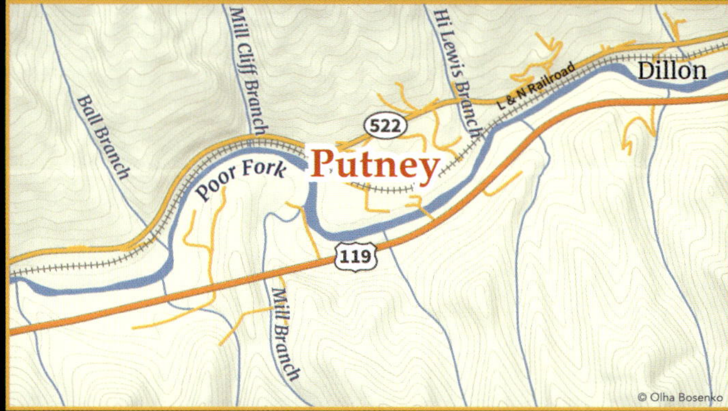

Inter-Mountain Coal & Lumber Co.

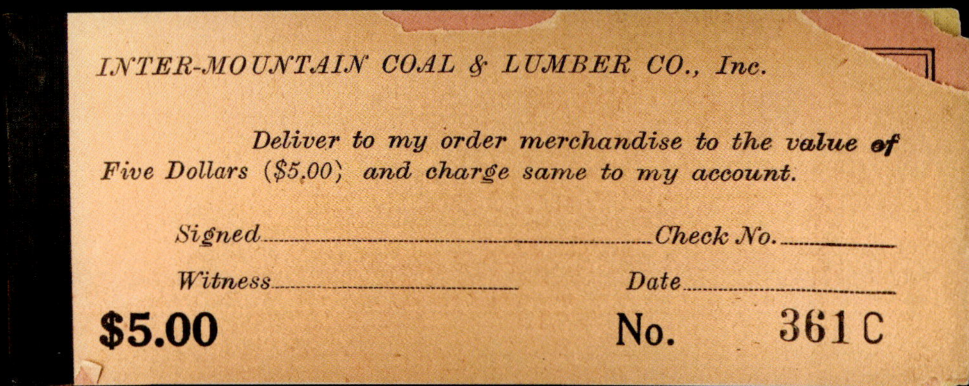
INTER-MOUNTAIN COAL & LUMBER CO., Inc.

Deliver to my order merchandise to the value of Five Dollars ($5.00) and charge same to my account.

Signed.................................... *Check No.*..........

Witness.................................... *Date*..........

$5.00 No. 361 C

The coupons in this book are good only for Merchandise and will not be replaced if lost. They are NOT TRANSFERABLE and will not be honored if detached from this book.

RAND MCNALLY & COMPANY, CHICAGO

THE COUPONS IN THIS BOOK ARE

GOOD FOR MERCHANDISE ONLY

AT THE STORE OF Inter-Mountain Coal & Lbr. Co., Inc.

$5.00

PATENTED JAN. 17TH, 1911

Issued to ______ *Check No.* ______

Issued by ______ Date ______

NOT TRANSFERABLE NOT GOOD IF DETACHED No. 361 C

Courtesy of Burley Williams

INTER - MOUNTAIN COAL & LUMBER CO.
MERCHANDISE ONLY
NOT GOOD IF DETACHED
866D
1 CENT
NOT TRANSFERABLE
INTER - MOUNTAIN COAL & LUMBER CO.
MERCHANDISE ONLY
NOT GOOD IF DETACHED
437D
2 CENTS
NOT TRANSFERABLE
INTER - MOUNTAIN COAL & LUMBER CO.
MERCHANDISE ONLY
NOT GOOD IF DETACHED
456D
5 CENTS
NOT TRANSFERABLE
INTER - MOUNTAIN COAL & LUMBER CO.
MERCHANDISE ONLY
NOT GOOD IF DETACHED
435D
10 CENTS
NOT TRANSFERABLE
INTER - MOUNTAIN COAL & LUMBER CO.
MERCHANDISE ONLY
NOT GOOD IF DETACHED
898D
25 CENTS
NOT TRANSFERABLE
INTER - MOUNTAIN COAL & LUMBER CO.
MERCHANDISE ONLY
NOT GOOD IF DETACHED
11D
2 CENTS
NOT TRANSFERABLE
TWO
ONE
INTER - MOUNTAIN COAL & LUMBER CO.
MERCHANDISE ONLY
NOT GOOD IF DETACHED
361C
25 CENTS
NOT TRANSFERABLE
TW'Y-FIVE
TEN
FIVE
TWO
ONE

Inter-Mountain Coal & Lumber Co. continued

Not shown: A10b, A10c

A5a
Brett Kennard

A5b
Howard Fortune

A10a

A25
Ken Allen

A50

A100
Eben Flood

B5
Frank Sutton

B10

Ridgeway
2403

Named for the Ridgeway Coal Co.

Harlan Coal & Coke Co.

Not shown: D100,

D1
Ken Allen

D5
Howard Fortune

D25
Howard Fortune

D50
Ken Allen

E1
Ken Allen

Harlan Coal and Coke Co. continued

E5
Howard Fortune

E10
Ken Allen

E25
Tommy Skeens

E100
Ken Allen

E50

D10

Harlan-Ridgeway Mining Co.

A5

A10
Claudia Piper

A25

A50

A100
Burley Williams

B10
Ken Allen

B50

B100

Ridgeway Coal Corporation

C5a

C5b
Ken Allen

C10a
Ken Allen

C10b
Steve Cawood

C10c
Ken Allen

C25

C50a
Ken Allen

C50b

C100
Ken Allen

Rue 2479

Also called Lenarue

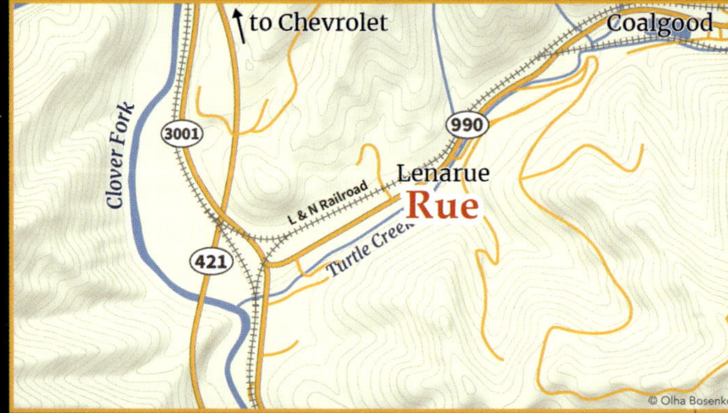

Southern-Harlan Coal Co.

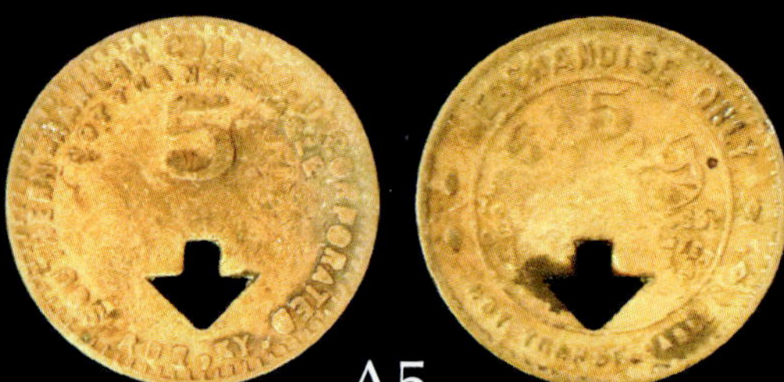

A5a
Ken Allen

A5b
Steve Cawood

A10a
Frank Sutton

A10b

A25
Ken Allen

A50

A100
Steve Cawood

B1

B5

B25

Frank Sutton

C1

Splint 2639

Earlier called Nolansburg.

Splint Coal Corporation

Paper scrip courtesy of Burley Williams

Stanfill 2651

Mahan-Ellison Coal Corp.

Not shown: D1b, D1c, D5b, E1, F25

A5

Howard Fortune

A10

Steve Cawood

A25

Steve Cawood

A50

A100

Mahan-Ellison Coal Corp. continued

B5a
Ken Allen

B5b
Steve Cawood

B10a
Ken Allen

B10b
Steve Cawood

B25
Frank Sutton

B50
Ken Allen

B100
Ken Allen

C5
Ron Saylor

C10

C25

C50

C100a
Ken Allen

C100b
Ken Allen

C100c
Steve Cawood

D1a
Ron Saylor

D5a
Ken Allen

Three Point

2789

Also called Coalville. Named for three nearby peaks, or, according to the Three Point Coal Co., the three virtues of dependability, service, and quality.

Three Point Coal Corp.

In 1943, 12 miners were killed in an explosion of the Harlan Seam at the Three Point mine, the second fatal explosion of this seam after the fatalities at the Zero Mine in 1932.

A1

B5

B10

B25

B50

B100

Ken Allen

Ken Allen

Totz 2817

Named for Harry Totz, owner of Harlan-Cumberland Coal Co.

Harlan Central Coal Company

A5
Steve Cawood

A10
David Mullins

A25
Steve Cawood

A50
Howard Fortune

A100
Ken Allen

B100

Ken Allen

Totz Coal Company, Inc.

Paper scrip courtesy of Burley Williams

Harlan-Cumberland Coal Mining Co.

C1
Howard Fortune

C5
Ken Allen

C10
Steve Cawood

C25
Steve Cawood

C50
Steve Cawood

C100
Howard Fortune

Twila 2853

Formerly known as Lowe or Low.

Creech Coal Co.

Not shown: B100, D5, D10, D25, D50, D100

A5b
Ken Allen

A5a

A10
Steve Cawood

A25
Steve Cawood

A50a

A50b
Steve Cawood

A100
Brett Kennard

B5

B10
Ken Allen

B25
Steve Cawood

C10
Steve Cawood

Verda 2893

Named for Verda Middleton, an early settler.

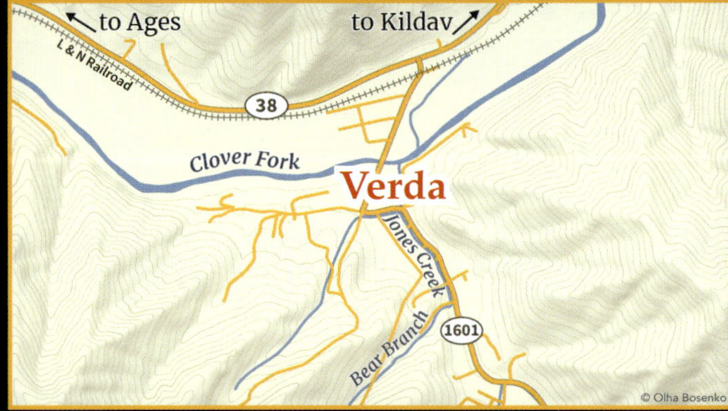

Wm. D. Boyer Trustee & Co. Bear Branch Mine

Not shown: J1, J5, J25

B50
Ken Allen

B100
David Mullins

C10
David Schenkman

C25
Ken Allen

C50
Ken Allen

C100
Steve Cawood

Harlan-Wallins Coal Co.

Not shown: A5b

A5a

A10
David Mullins

A25
Howard Fortune

A50a

A50b
Steve Cawood

F5

F10
Frank Sutton

F25a

F50

F25b

Harlan-Wallins Coal Co. continued

G5

Sunshine Grocery Company

I1

Tommy Skeens

I5

I10

David Mullins

I25

Howard Fortune

I50

Tommy Skeens

I50

Ken Allen

Verda Supply Co.

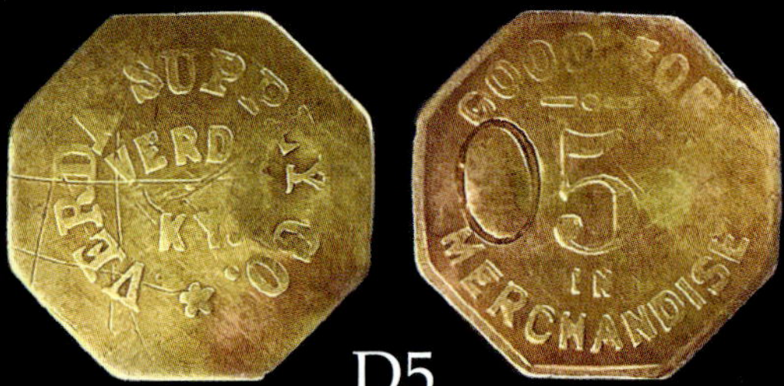

D5

Steve Cawood

D10

Steve Cawood

D25

Ken Allen

D100

Steve Cawood

E5

Howard Fortune

E10

E25

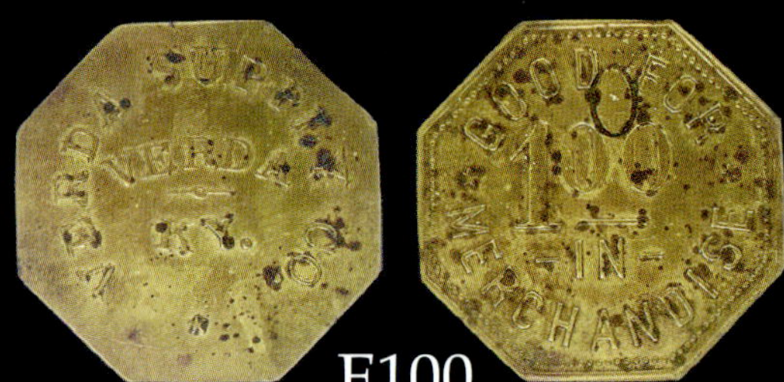

E100

Howard Fortune

H5
Ken Allen

H10
Ken Allen

H25
Burley Williams

H50

Ken Allen

Brett Kennard

In 1931, Fred Lester and three of his relatives were charged with murder in the poisoning death of Mr. Lester's employee, Lonnie Prince, on whom Mr. Lester had a $20,000 insurance policy taken out shortly before his death. One of the Lester boys had bought strychnine at Pierce's Drug Store in Evarts just before the death. When the Lesters agreed to testify for the prosecution in the Battle of Evarts case, the murder charges were dropped.

D25

Ken Allen

HARLAN-WALLINS COAL
CORPORATION
50
INCORPORATED
WH
VERDA, KY.

F50

HARLAN-WALLINS COAL
CORPORATION
50
INCORPORATED
WH
VERDA, KY.

Wallins 2929

Wallins is named for Wallins Creek, itself named for an early Virginia surveyor.

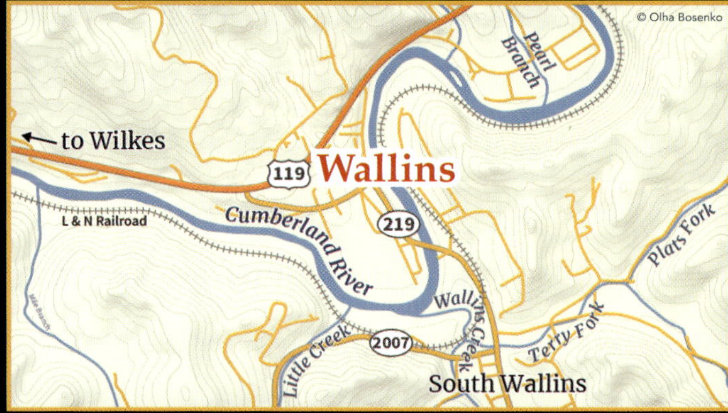

The Good Coal Co. Inc.

Not shown: D5, D25, D50, E1

B500
Ken Allen

C5
Steve Cawood

C10
Steve Cawood

C25
Steve Cawood

C50
Howard Fortune

C100
Howard Fortune

D10

Ken Allen

D100

Howard Fortune

F1

I1

Utilities Coal Corporation

Not shown: G100

G500

NIck Fugate & Shawn Fugate

Wallins Creeks Coal Co. Incorporated

Not shown: J5, L5, L25, N10, N50

A5
Ken Allen

J10a

J10b
Steve Cawood

J25
Brett Kennard

K5a
Brett Kennard

K5b
Brett Kennard

K10
Ken Allen

K25
Ken Allen

K50

K100
Howard Fortune

L10
Ken Allen

L50

Wallins Creek Collieries

M1
Steve Cawood

K25
Ken Allen

L10

Ken Allen

White Star
3011

Formerly called Day, after a local family. Later Dayhoit and Wilhoit after Roy Wilhoit, the founder of a coal mine.

White Star Coal Co.

A5
Ken Allen

A10
Steve Cawood

A25

A50

Wilkes 3034

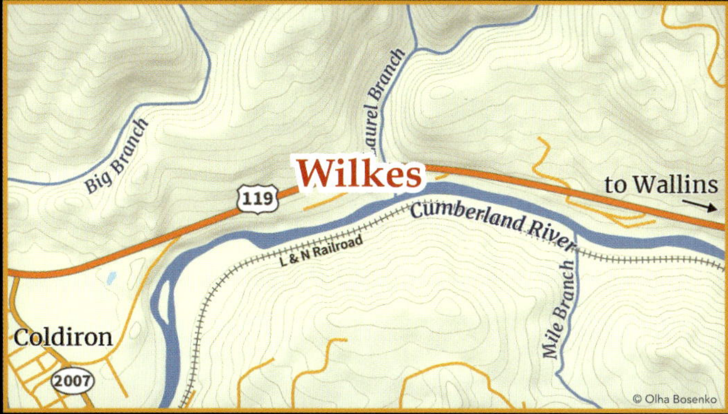

Harlan Block Coal Co.

Not shown: A5

Yancey 3109

Harlan Fuel Co.

A1
Howard Fortune

A5a
Ken Allen

A5b
Brett Kennard

A5c
Steve Cawood

A10
Ken Allen

A25
Howard Fortune

A50
Frank Sutton

A100a
David Mullins

A100b
David Mullins

B500

C5
Ken Allen

C10
Ken Allen

C25
Ken Allen

Yancey Store

Not shown: E5

D5
Ken Allen

D10

D25

D50

D100

D500

E100
Ken Allen

Explosives control tokens and light token courtesy of Ken Allen

In 1932, Harlan Fuel's Zero Mine exploded, killing 23 miners. The Kentucky Bureau of Mines report said that the cause was exploding coal dust, triggered by blasting, and that the mine was covered throughout by fine coal dust that had not been treated with rock dust or watered down. The inspector required Harlan Fuel to stop using open-flame carbide lamps and to use battery-operated lights instead. The company then required miners to rent a lamp and used these tokens to control their use.

ACKNOWLEDGMENTS

The officers and members of the National Scrip Collectors Association (scripcollectors.org), including President Lynn Ours and Secretary Garrett Salyers, have supported this project from the beginning and I am grateful for their help.

Kevin Andersen, the editor of Scrip Talk, the club's newsletter, worked unfailingly to get the word out about the need for photographs of scarce scrip.

The late Frank Sutton was among the first collectors to share large numbers of photographs of his scrip.

Burley Williams has been unfailingly helpful with knowledge and advice about scrip and coal mining in Bell and Harlan counties. His unmatched collection of paper scrip is presented in these pages. Burley and Stella Williams welcomed me into their home and Burley gave me access to his large and varied collection. His early help was invaluable, getting this project underway when it floundered. His unmatched collection of paper scrip is presented in these pages.

Thanks to Ken Allen who sent me photo after photo from his unequaled collection, and whose scrip photographs are the best I have seen.

Steve and Sissy Cawood welcomed me into their home for photograph sessions and discussions that always taught me more about Harlan County. Steve's knowledge of Harlan County and coal mining is extensive and he willingly shared it.

David Mullins was an early supporter of the project and provided several important photographs.

Howard Fortune allowed me to photograph his extensive collection, where I found many rare pieces.

Ron Saylor let me photograph his previously unknown paper scrip covers from U.S. Steels' mine at Lynch.

Tommy Skeens sent photographs of several scrip dimes and dollars that I saw nowhere else.

Brett Kennard was very generous with his collection.

Billy Campbell is extremely knowledgeable about scrip and was always willing to share.

Thanks to Neal Burton for moral support.

For sending me otherwise unobtainable photographs, I am grateful to David Schenkman, Frank Yunyon, Steve Calwell, Steve Hayden, Nick Fugate, Shawn Fugate, John Slusher, Tim Howard, the Louisville Numismatic Exchange, and Randy Salyers.

To the guardians of Portal 31, the miners museum at Lynch, Kentucky, Mike and MaryJo O'Bradovich: Thank you for information about all things Lynch.

Thanks to David Bowling, Sr., for his photographs and research about the lethal aspects of Harlan's private deputy system.

Thanks to Ellie Piper for early help with editing.

Thanks to Cecil Bothwell and Francine Cavanaugh for help with research.

I want to thank my friend Anita Cava for suggesting this project.

Starr Sariego's photographs of the Harlan Miners Memorial helped illustrate the human cost of coal mining.

Olha Bosenko's excellent maps kept us all oriented.

Peggy Stockdale designed the book and its cover, set the type and wrangled the photographs into the right places. Her professionalism, hard work and good sense improved it all.

Thanks to my editor, Peter Gregutt, who questioned everything. His suggestions were always helpful and left the book in much better shape than he found it.

Most of all, my thanks to my wife, Laura, for her unfailing support for this project.

ENDNOTES

1 Harry M. Caudill, *Theirs Be the Power: The Moguls of Eastern Kentucky* (Urbana:University of Illinois Press, 1983) 88–90.
2 John W. Hevener, *Which Side Are You On?: The Harlan County Coal Miners. 1931–39* (Urbana: University of Illinois Press, 1978) 3.
3 Ibid.
4 Alessandro Portelli, *They Say in Harlan County: An Oral History* (Oxford: Oxford University Press, 2011) 101.
5 Ibid, p. 102.
6 Caudill, *Theirs Be the Power,* 93-95.
7 Robert M. Rennick, *Kentucky Place Names* (Lexington, The University Press of Kentucky, 1984) 169.
8 Forrest McDonald, *Insull: The Rise and Fall of a Billionaire Utility Tycoon* (Washington, D.C., 1962) 332.
9 John Greenway, *American Folk Songs of Protest* (Philadelphis, University of Pennsylvania Press, 1953) 150.
10 Hal King, "Kenvir Coal Warms the South Pole," Paper Presented to the Athenaeum Society, March 7, 2013.
11 Porticelli, 119.
12 Ibid.
13 Black Mountain Corp. v. Appleman, 33 S.W.2d 327 (Ky. Ct. App. 1930).
14 Theodore Dreiser, et. al., *Harlan Miners Speak: Report on Terrorism in the Kentucky Coal Fields* (Lexington: The University of Kentucky Press, 1932) 30.
15 Hevener, 22.
16 Michael Ruth, *Memory of a Miner: A true-life story from Harlan County's heyday* (Knoxville, Growth Resourcees, 2014) 155.
17 William H. Turner, *The Harlan Renaissance* (Morgantown: West Virginia University Press, 2021) 145.
18 William D. Forester, *Harlan County: The Turbulent Thirties* (1986) 132.
19 Elyssa East, "The Ballad of Harlan County," *Oxford American*, Issue 93, July 11, 2016.
20 Robert L. Stevens and Jared A. Fogel, "From Mountain Men to Miners," *Social Education*, Vol.63, September 1999.
21 Hevener, 8.
22 Ibid., 84.
23 Ibid., 16.

24 Ibid., 17.
25 Ibid.
26 G.W. Hilton, "The Truck Act of 1831," *The Economic History Review*, Vol. 10, No. 3 (1958) 470.
27 Ibid.
28 Ibid., 471.
29 Stuart E. Brown, *Scrip: Trade Tokens Issued by United States Coal Mining Companies and Company Stores* (Virginia Book Company) 43.
30 Article 1, Section 8, *U.S. Constitution.*
31 Daniel Bringer, John Adams, *The Law of Mines and Mining in the United States* (Boston, Little, Brown, 1897) 769.
32 Report to the President on the Anthracite Coal Strike of May-October, 1902.
33 Quoted in Eric R. Schena and David E. Schenkman, "The System Scrip Makers of Western Ohio," *TAMS Journal*, Sept./Oct. 2016, Vol. LVI, No. 5, Part 2.
34 Illustration reproduced in Brown, 175.
35 Jim Garland, *Welcome the Traveler Home: Jim Garland's Story of the Kentucky Mountains* (Lexington: The University Press of Kentucky, 1983) 133.
36 Henever, 62.
37 Carletta A. Bush, *Faith, Power, and Conflict: Miner Preachers and the United Mine Workers of America in the Harlan County Mine Wars, 1931-1939* (West Virginia University, 2006, Doctoral Dissertation) 74.
38 Ibid.
39 Ibid., 95.
40 Hevener, 33.
41 Bush, 34.
42 Hevener, 34.
43 Ibid., 35.
44 Ibid., 11.
45 Quoted in John Dos Passos, "Harlan: Working under the Gun," *The New Republic,* December 2, 1931, 66.
46 Greenway, 158.
47 Ibid., 167.
48 Garland, 138.
49 Portelli, 41.
50 Hevener, 41.
51 *New York Times*, September 29, 1931, 1.
52 Ibid., 46.
53 Ibid.
54 Ibid., 75.
55 Ibid., 133.
56 Ruth, 85–105.
57 Robert Shogan, *The Battle of Blair Mountain* (New York, Basic Books, 2004).
58 George J. Titler, *Hell in Harlan* (Beckley, WV, 1972), 6.
59 Hevener, 56.
60 Ibid., 55.
61 Ibid., 57.

62 Ibid., 60.
63 Ibid., 61.
64 Ketchel Carey, "Which Side Are You On," July 15, 2020. www.ilr.cornell.edu/buffalo-co-lab/high-road/which-side-are-you/
65 Tom Maxwell, "A History of American Protest Music: Which Side Are You On?" *Longreads*, August 2018. longreads.com/2018/08/29/history-of-american-protest-music-which-side-are-you-on/
66 Garland, 149.
67 Ibid., 184.
68 Ibid., 155.
69 Hevener, 63.
70 Garland, 167.
71 Havener, 114.
72 Theodore Dreiser, et. al., *Harlan Miners Speak: Report on Terrorism in the Kentucky Coal Fields* (Lexington, KY, University Press of Kentucky, 1932).
73 Thomas N. Bethell, "Contract at Brookside" (1976).
74 Hevener, 18.
75 Titler, 101.
76 Hevener, 142.
77 Correspondence with David Bowling, Sr.
78 *Louisville Courier-Journal*, May 15, 1938.
79 Hevener, 146.
80 *Louisville Courier-Journal*, May 25, 1938.
81 Hevener, 150-51.
82 Ibid., 151.
83 Ibid., 181.
84 Bonnie E. Stewart, No. 9: The 1968 Farmington Mine Disaster (Morgantown: West Virginia University Press, 2012) 1.
85 CNN Editorial Research, "US Mine Disaster Fast Facts." www.cnn.com/2013/07/13/us/u-s-mine-disasters-fast-facts/index.html
86 Shaunna L. Scott, *Two Sides to Everything: The Cultural construction of Class Consciousness in Harlan County*, Kentucky (Albany: State Univeristy of New York Press) 199.
87 Scott, 210.
88 Ibid., 211.
89 Ibid.
90 Ibid., 209.
91 Scott, 212.
92 Hevener, 77.
93 Ibid, 132.
94 Ibid, 158-170.
95 Lyrics by Merle Travis, © Warner Chappell Music, Inc.
96 Song by Jean Richie.

Welcome the Traveler Home
KENTUCKY
Memory of a Miner
Dr. Michael Ruth
WHICH SIDE ARE YOU ON? · THOMAS GEOGHEGAN
Greenberg
A Circle of Trust: Remembering SNCC
SCOTT
KENTUCKY Place Names
AMERICAN FOLKSONGS OF PROTEST
FORGOTTEN BOOKS
SOFT COAL, HARD CHOICES
FISHBACK
OXFORD
BEFORE WE FORGET
FORESTER
Unearthing Seeds of Fire: The Idea of Highlander by Frank Adams
BLAIR
INSULL
FORREST McDONALD
BLACK LUNG
CAUDILL THEIRS BE THE POWER
UNIVERSITY OF ILLINOIS PRESS
My Appalachia
Caudill
APPALACHIAN RECKONING
Weiner Coalfield Jews AN APPALACHIAN HISTORY
ILLINOIS
Dick Weissman Which Side Are You On?
Portelli THEY SAY IN HARLAN COUNTY
OXFORD
CARAWAN VOICES FROM THE MOUNTAINS GEORGIA
Hevener Which Side Are You On?
THE Battle OF BLAIR MOUNTAIN
SHOGAN
Harry M. Caudill
NIGHT COMES TO THE CUMBERLANDS
Bloody Harlan
WILKERSON TO LIVE HERE, YOU HAVE TO FIGHT
THE COURT-MARTIAL OF MOTHER JONES
ANDREWS Killing for Coal
AMERICA'S DEADLIEST LABOR WAR
Ward and Rogers
CONVICTS, COAL, and the BANNER MINE TRAGEDY
Shifflett Coal Towns
TENNESSEE
Which Side Are You On? Lynda Ann Ewen Vanguard Books
GEORGE J. TITLER
THE HARLAN RENAISSANCE Turner
Harlan County—The Turbulent Thirties
William D. Forester
BOYER MORAIS
LABOR'S UNTOLD STORY
THE QUIET SICKNESS EARL DOTTER
PRISCILLA LONG WHERE THE SUN NEVER SHINES
F.D.R. His Personal Letters
EARLY YEARS
No.9 THE 1968 FARMINGTON MINE DISASTER
BONNIE E. STEWART
HEVENER Which Side Are You On? The Harlan County Coal Miners, 1931–39
20,000 COAL COMPANY STORES

BIBLIOGRAPHY

Books:

Adams, Frank with Myles Horton. *Unearthing Seeds of Fire: The Idea of Highlander*. Durham, NC: John F. Blair, 1975.

Boyer, Richard O. and Herbert M. Morais. *Labor's Untold Story*. Pittsburg: United Electrical, Radio & Machine Workers of America, 1955.

Buckley, Geoffrey L. *Extracting Appalachia: Images of the Consolidation Coal Company, 1910-1945*. Athens: Ohio University Press, 2004.

Carawan, Candie and Guy Candie. *Voices from the Mountains: The People of Appalachia–Their Faces, Their Words, Their Songs*. Athens: The University of Georgia Press, 1996.

Caudill, Harry M. *Night Comes to the Cumberlands: A Biography of a Depressed Area*, Ashland, Kentucky: Jesse Stuart Foundation, 1963.

Caudill, Harry M. *Theirs Be the Power: The Moguls of Eastern Kentucky*, Urbana: University of Illinois Press, 1983.

Caudill, Rebecca, *My Appalachia, A Reminiscence*. New York: Holt, Rinehart and Winston, 1966.

Derickson, Alan. *Black Lung: Anatomy of a Public Health Disaster*. Ithaca: Cornell University Press, 1998.

Dodrill, Gordon. *20,000 Coal Company Stores*. Pittsburg: 1971.

Dotter, Earl. *The Quiet Sickness: A Photographic Chronicle of Hazardous Work in America*. Fairfax, WV: American Industrial Hygiene Association, 1998.

Dreiser, Theodore, et al. *Harlan Miners Speak, Report on Terrorism in the Kentucky Coal Fields*. Lexington: University of Kentucky Press, 1932.

Edkins, Donald O. *Edkins' Catalogue of Coal Company Store Scrip*. The National Scrip Collectors Association, 1977.

Ewen, Lynda Ann, *Which Side Are You On?: The Brookside Mine Strike in Harlan County, Kentucky, 1973-1974*. Chicago: Vangard Books, 1979.

Fishback, Price V. *Soft Coal, Hard Choices: The Economic Welfare of Bituminous Coal Miners, 1890-1930*. New York: Oxford University Press, 1992.

Forester, William D. *Before We Forget, Harlan County: 1920 Through 1930*. 1983.

Forester, William D. *Harlan County: The Turbulent Thirties*. 1986.

Garland, Jim. *Welcome the Traveler Home: Jim Garland's Story of the Kentucky Mountains*. Lexington: The University Press of Kentucky, 1983.

Greenberg, Cheryl Lynn, ed. *A Circle of Trust: Remembering SNCC*. New Brunswick: Rutgers University Press, 1998.

Greenway, John. *American Folksongs of Protest*. Philadelphia: University of Pennsylvania Press, 1953.

Harkins, Anthony and Meredith McCarroll, eds. *Appalachian Reckoning: A Region Responds to Hillbilly Elegy*. Morgantown: West Virginia University Press, 2019.

Hevener, John W. *Which Side Are You On?: The Harlan County Coal Miners, 1931-39*. Urbana: University of Illinois Press, 1978.

Long, Priscilla. *Where the Sun Never Shines: A History of America's Bloody Coal Industry*. New York: Paragon House, 1989.

McDonald, Forrest. *Insull: The Rise and Fall of a Billionaire Utility Tycoon*. Washington, D.C.: 1962.

Portelli, Alexandro. *They Say in Harlan County: An Oral History*. Oxford: Oxford University Press, 2011.

Rennick, Robert M. *Kentucky Place Names*. Lexington: The University Press of Kentucky, 1984.

Romalls, Shelly. *Pistol Packin' Mama: Aunt Molly Jackson and the Politics of Folksong*. Urbana: University of Illinois Press, 1999.

Roosevelt, Elliott, ed. *FDR: His Personal Letters: Early Years*. New York: Duell, Sloan & Pearce, 1948.

Ruth, Michael. *Memory of a Miner: A True-Life Story from Harlan County's Heyday*. Knoxville: Growth Resources.

Salyers, Garrett and Mike Williams, eds. *Edkins' Catalogue of Coal Company Store Scrip, Fourth Edition, Volume I*. Olive Hill, KY: The National Scrip Collectors Association, 2015.

Scott, Shaunna L. *Two Sides to Everything: The Cultural Construction of Class Consciousness in Harlan County Kentucky*. Albany: State University of New York Press, 1995.

Shogan, Robert. *The Battle of Blair Mountain: The Story of America's Largest Labor Uprising*. New York: Basic Books, 2004.

Shifflett, Crandall A. *Coal Towns: Life, Work, and Culture in Company Towns of Southern Appalachia, 1880–1960*. Knoxville: The University of Tennessee Press, 1991.

Steel, Edward M. Jr., ed. *The Court-Martial of Mother Jones*. Lexington: The University Press of Kentucky, 1995.

Taylor, Paul F. *Bloody Harlan: The United Mine Workers of America in Harlan County, Kentucky, 1931–1941*. St. Martin, Ohio: Commonwealth Book Company, 1990.

Turner, William H. *The Harlan Renaissance: Stories of Black Life in Appalachian Coal Towns*. Morgantown: West Virginia University Press, 2021.

Weiner, Deborah R. *Coalfield Jews, An Appalachian History*. Urbana: University of Illinois Press, 2006.

Weissman, Dick. *Which Side Are You On?: An Inside History of the Folk Music Revival in America*. New York: Continuum, 2005.

Wilkerson, Jessica. *To Live Here, You Have to Fight: How Women Led Appalachian Movements for Social Justice*. Urbana, University of Illinois Press, 2019.

Ward, Robert David and William Warren Rogers. *Convicts, Coal, and the Banner Mine Tragedy*. Tuscaloosa: The University of Alabama Press, 1987.

Dissertation:

Bush, Carletta A. *Faith, Power, and Conflict: Miner Preachers and the United Mine Workers of America in the Harlan County Mine Wars, 1931—1939*. Morgantown: West Virginia University, 2006.

Periodical:

Schena, Eric R. and David E. Schenkman. "The System Scrip Makers of Western Ohio." *TAMS Journal*, Sept./Oct. 2016.

Hearings

The La Follette Committee. U.S. Senate Hearings on Conditions in Coal Fields in Harlan and Bell Counties, Kentucky. appalachiancenter.as.uky.edu/sites/default/files/HD9547_KA4.pdf

INDEX

Leslie County
Beech Fork
Pine Mounta
Straight Creek
Putney
Cumberland River
White Star
Harlan
Black Joe
Brookside
Ages Creek
Evart
Kilday
Drape
Kitts
Coxton
Ages
Verda
Malcomson
Gaston
Jones Cre
Wallins
Wilkes
Molus
Path Fork
Wallins Creek
Ewing Creek
Bland
Elcomb
Grays Knob
Chevrolet
Martins Fork
Coalgood
Lowe
Lenarue (Rue)
Crummies Cre
Foresters Creek
Kentenia
Lisle
Banner Fork
Twila
Banner Fork
Mary Alice
Cawood
Crummies
Bobs Creek
Stanfill
Yancey
Catron Creek
Three Point
Bardo
Liggett
Martins Fork Lake
Cranks Cr
Bell County
Insull
Path Fork
Alva
Puckett Creek
Mill Creek
Lick Branch
Brownies Creek
Cumberland
N
0 1 2 3